BEYOND HUMAN

Praise For *Beyond Human*

"Jaden's book *Beyond Human* is brilliant! It provides easily accessed concepts and practices designed to take us beyond our limits. This book is your invitation to make magical living your everyday reality. I highly recommend it."

REV. JOSHUA HEARTSONG, SPIRITUAL DIRECTOR,
THE CENTER OF LIGHT AND TRUTH, BOULDER, CO

"The universe is always on our side, flowing through us, living through us, <u>as</u> us. In *Beyond Human*, Jaden shows us how to stop fighting the flow. She presents a delightful collection of effective techniques to guide us out of the contracted eddies of our programmed thoughts and perceptions back into the flow of our own universal health and joyful intelligence."

JACK ELIAS, CHT, AUTHOR OF *FINDING TRUE MAGIC: TRANSPERSONAL HYPNOSIS & HYPNOTHERAPY/NLP.*
DIRECTOR, AMERICAN INSTITUTE FOR TRANSPERSONAL HYPNOTHERAPY/NLP, AND LUCID HEART THERAPY & LIFE COACHING, HTTP://FINDINGTRUEMAGIC.COM

"Beyond Human invites us to go deeper into the essence of who we really are, with the perfect balance of expanded consciousness and grounded practicality. This is a book I want all my clients to read as they embark on their journey to the deep masculine."

"The message is simple: You ARE a miracle and you CAN create miracles. *Beyond Human* is a masterful guidebook with practical wisdom, playful insights, and powerful tools that assist us in accessing the realm of all possibilities."

"Don't we all wonder if being human is 'enough?' While we are divine at heart, some days underscore only the limitations of this humbling existence. Jaden's book, *Beyond Human*, is one of the few to short-circuit negativity and the murky qualities of our existence to help us explore the power, beauty, and miracles of being human."

BEYOND
HUMAN

CLAIMING THE POWER
AND MAGIC OF YOUR
LIMITLESS SELF

JADEN ROSE PHOENIX

Cherryhurst Press
Seattle, Washington

Cherryhurst Press
P.O. Box 75451
Seattle, WA 98175

Cherryhurst Press is a division of Divine Life Technologies, LLC

Note to the reader: This book is intended as an informational guide. The remedies, approaches, and techniques described herein are meant to supplement, and not to be a substitute for, professional medical care or treatment. They should not be used to treat a serious ailment without prior consultation with a qualified health care professional.

Printed and bound in the United States.

10   9   8   7   6   5   4   3   2   1

Cover design by 1106 Design
Back cover copy by Write to Your Market
Text design and layout by Virginia Scott Bowman
This book was typeset in Garamond Premier Pro and Gill Sans with Arepo, Trajan Pro, and Gill Sans used as display typefaces.

for all Beings,
especially Toby,
the truest angel of light

CONTENTS

Acknowledgments   xi

Introduction: Becoming Your Own Guru   1

PART ONE
∽
EXPANDING CONSCIOUSNESS: BECOMING LIMITLESS

1 Rules to Live By   6

Redefining Human   7

Feeling Inadequate Doesn't Matter   13

    Tip: Using Meta Rule Sets   13

    Exercise: Creating Your Meta-Rules   20

The Limitations of Mind   21

    Tip: Learning to Move Your Consciousness   22

2 The Basics of Expanding Consciousness   24

Begin Where You Can Begin   24

Find Joy First   27

Gathering Yourself to Begin   28

    Exercise: Gathering Yourself   30

Getting Out of Your Head   31
    Exercise: Moving into Your Heart-Space   32
Advanced Awareness Exercises   33
    Exercise: Moving through Your Bodies   34
    Exercise: Moving Up and Down   35
Discovering the Big You   37
    Tip: You Are Not Your Thoughts   37
    Tip: Gaining Leverage with Your Emotions   39
    Exercise: Dispersing the Emotional Vortex   42

3 Mapping the Territory of Consciousness   44
Basic Maps   44
Finding the Present Now   45
    Exercise: Discovering the Space Between   46
    Exploring from the Present   47
    What's the Catch?   48
    From Present to Where?   48
    Exercise: Visiting the Lower World   49
Other Maps for Unseen Worlds   51
Making Your Own Map   52
    Tips for Making Your Own Map   52
    An Alternate Map Technique   53
    Mapping Your Middle World   54
    Question, Explore, Invent, Experiment   54

4 Finding the Place of Power   56
The Point of Power   56
It Happens When You Least Suspect   59
Fearology   61
    Fear is not Your Identity   63
    Future Fear   65

Moving beyond Fear 66

    The Illusion of Fear 67

        Exercise: Fear-Busting Rehearsal 69

        Exercise: Seeing through the Illusion of Fear 70

PART TWO

PLAYING WITH CONSCIOUSNESS: CHANGING YOURSELF AND YOUR WORLD

5 Expanding Your Personal Power 78

Hearing Your Guidance 79

    Exercise: Choosing from Your Heart 86

Tips for Hearing Your Guides 88

    Exercise: Strengthening Your Connection to Guidance 89

What Happens Once You Hear Your Guides? 90

Should You Fire Your Guides? 95

The Guru Is Dead 97

6 Using Consciousness to Create Health 102

The Alchemical Container 106

Everything Exists as a Pattern 107

Holographic Healing 108

The Basics of Finding a Pattern 110

    Exercise: Finding Patterns 112

Consciousness and Intent 112

Calibration of Results 115

    Exercise: Changing a Health Pattern 116

7 Using Consciousness to Create Financial Freedom   119

Creating an Immediate Shift   120

Seeing Your Patterns   120

    Exercise: Shifting Your Money Patterns   121

The Power of Gratitude   123

    Exercise: Gratitude Meditation   124

The Morphic Field of Money   127

    Exercise: Detaching from Morphic Fields   129

Finding Alternatives   130

    Exercise: Finding a New Option   132

    Exercise: Moving beyond Your Circle of Awareness   133

8 Using Consciousness to Create Great Relationships   136

Connecting to Source   139

    Exercise: Completing Your Own Circuits   140

    Exercise: The Mirror   142

Shifting the Patterns that Hold Us Back from Love   143

    *Exercise: Changing the Patterns that Keep
    You from Love*   144

Vibrating into Love   146

    Exercise: Becoming the Vibration You Seek   147

Afterword: Expanding Consciousness beyond
the Personal   149

An Unexpected Gift   150

From Separation to Unified Consciousness   151

Appendix: Quick Reference Guide to Exercises   154

Bibliography   158

About the Author   161

ACKNOWLEDGMENTS

I would like to thank those who helped me along the amazing and sometimes arduous path of creating this book. First, I would have gotten nowhere without the repeated admonishments from David Cates to just give up on the book and spend time having fun. I sure showed him! However when it became obvious that this book was going to happen, he gave me priceless (and honest!) feedback on my drafts.

I'd also like to thank my patient coach and fellow author, Kim Olver. I relied on her experiences and could not have negotiated this process without her. Others who also provided valuable help and input are Judy Zeigler and my exceptional editor, Despina Gurlides.

Of course, I must thank Richard Bartlett for showing me, through ridiculous example, the value of having fun. And Mark Dunn, through equally ridiculous example, taught me the value of experimentation. Imagine the scene: "Hey, you got your fun in my experimentation!" "No, you got your experimentation on my fun!" "Oh, wait! That's magically delicious!"

I happily thank all the clients, students and participants in my programs—all of you are my greatest teachers, and many of you urged me for years to write this book. And finally, I was lucky to have the support and encouragement of my parents during this process. Deepest gratitude to all!

BECOMING YOUR OWN GURU

There is nothing special about me. I'm just an ordinary person like you. If I can navigate my way through expanding my consciousness, then you can too. I've read the other books. Many of these amazing teachers all had something noteworthy or special about them: either their mother heard angels calling their name at the moment of their birth, or they were saved by angels in a high speed crash—you get the idea. If that's what was required to become a guru, to learn to wield the power of consciousness, then I had no hope.

I had not experienced visitors in angelic or alien form. I didn't see auras. I had never healed myself, or anyone else, spontaneously. I was just average and ordinary. While I thought I had a fairly well-managed life, I actually had spent most of it in a deep depression. I came to the beginnings of my consciousness work with many fears, issues, and above all, a lack of trust and a need to control everything, none of which were going to make things easy! But one trait I did have that may have served me early on was a tenacity unusual for most people. I always believed that I could learn anything. But no one was able to tell me *how* to learn to master my consciousness.

It's easy to get discouraged when you don't know what you're doing or how to do it. It seems that everybody else can do things better than you! This is the place where most of us usually begin, unless we've been saved by angels or had a near-death experience. How does an ordinary person come into great personal power by expanding their consciousness? This book explores just this question.

I will tell you how expanding my consciousness happened for me, which may or may not be useful for you. You will have your own way of getting there. The irony is that I could tell you not to look at my words but to look within yourself, because your answers are all within. But, right now, you are in that beginning place, looking outside of yourself to find the answers. Perhaps as you read my story, my words will begin to transform you so that you can believe that you have the answers you need. I will share with you the tricks and tips that helped me shift and expand my consciousness. Use what works for you, and remember that this is not the only way.

If you're reading this book, you already know the end of this story. The starting point might sound a little like you. Maybe you're just a regular person, living a normal life, but you have an inkling that there is something more; and so you're looking around for evidence that there is more to this human life. Perhaps you picked up this book because you have watched me work, or heard some of my lectures, or someone told you this book might help.

Yes, I did end up creating a wonderful life, full of joy and amazement. And yes, I seem to be one of those lucky people who has more leverage over her reality than most people can claim. However the story of how I accomplished this may totally surprise you. Some of it might seem similar to other books or cds on the topic of "creating your reality." But other parts of my story will fly in the face of "accepted" methods and philosophies. All I really want to share with you is *my* understanding of how I accomplished such leverage. Please keep in mind that this is just my experience, and not meant to be a dogma or prescription for you. Again, while you will find the ideas contained in this book very useful, ultimately you'll have to find your own path.

PART ONE

EXPANDING
CONSCIOUSNESS

BECOMING LIMITLESS

1

RULES TO LIVE BY

In the past, ascended masters, pharaohs, and saints had spiritual gifts and/or supernatural powers. These days we accept specially chosen holy men, shamans, and the like as having certain abilities to perform miracle healings. We also have psychics and mediums, who are not generally well respected by our western society. Though we may acknowledge that they have gifts, we hardly aspire to become like them.

Today, when "normal" people have healing tools or skills that seem a bit supernatural, we look for the myth of what sets them apart from a "regular" person. Perhaps angels attended their birth; or they had a dangerous experience that they were miraculously saved from; or they were struck by lightning or had a similar near death experience. We believe that such circumstances are needed to acquire magic powers of healing, telepathy, or the like. However we can all access these types of gifts, easily and naturally. They are not just for special people anymore. They are for everyone. Indeed, as our species evolves, we are able to tap into these skills more and more easily.

This book will teach you tools that you can use to expand your consciousness and develop what often seem like super powers to the uninitiated.

REDEFINING HUMAN

First things first: To develop these super power abilities, we need to put away our old ideas of how being human works. We need to suspend our beliefs and expectations about who we are, about our potential (as opposed to the potential of "special people"), and about what we need to do. But how can we just put all that aside?

Already you may be hearing doubts creep into your head or you may be thinking of ways you can fail. If I told you the truth—which is that you cannot possibly fail—you will perhaps think I'm insane. You may think you're failing if it isn't immediately obvious to you how to make yourself rich, beautiful, and famous with the first flick of your proverbial consciousness wand. However we are all in the process of shifting to something that is beyond human, of embracing a limitless Self. As Walt Whitman wrote: "I am large; I contain multitudes." He was right—we humans are capable of so much more than we've ever given ourselves credit for. And to do so, I hope you are ready to let go of some of your old ways of thinking.

Chances are you've been hearing a lot lately about how you can create and manifest your experiences with just your thoughts. Most people have heard of the Law of Attraction, and so enroll themselves in conscious language programs, and begin to post their affirmations everywhere. While becoming more aware of how words unconsciously structure reality is useful, creating a new reality requires more than just changing the words we use. It's actually simpler than that, though a somewhat complex discussion is needed to explain how manifesting can be simple, and why some of the more accepted beliefs about creating don't actually work well for most people.

The information about manifesting is not incorrect *per se*. However the main key is not so easy to put into words. Thus metaphysical teachers approximate the closest description that they can, which is sometimes not enough to achieve the required results.

While I can't guarantee that my description will allow you to manifest all your desires, it may add a component that was missing in your process or awareness. With this additional information and some of your own curiosity and experimentation, you will get closer to your unique path. But I cannot stress enough, that you will have to be active in this exploration! I can't spoon-feed you the answers! It's really up to you. So get excited and explore. Please don't get discouraged if following my instructions doesn't always work. Get curious! Experiment with the concept, play, and suspend judgment. I know you will find the path that will work for you!

Again, no one can do it for you. This, of course, is the ultimate downer for so many of us who were educated in the western style of regurgitated information. After teaching in the community college and university systems for so long, I can tell you where our education system has failed. We encourage students to memorize loads of information. While we do teach some problem solving skills, we only provide students with the tools to come up with the one correct answer. Rarely do we encourage young people to experiment and explore to obtain the answer that works for them.

Over and over again in seminars where I presented material, participants have asked me, "Can I use this with animals?" Or, "Could this work on my finances?" Or even, "Can I solve the climate warming problem with this?" And then, if the answer is, "Yes, you can use this on your finances," the questions to follow are, "How I can use this to improve my finances? What are the steps? Tell me how!" Now what's curious to me is how many people are willing to leave these answers up to *me*! They want *me* to tell them what they can or cannot do! Seriously, this worries me greatly. Question for yourself, experiment for yourself. My response to these types of questions is always, "Why not try and see what *you* can do?"

If I tell you to follow three steps that will make you rich, and you follow them religiously and don't become rich, then you are likely going to assume either a) you did it wrong, or b) the method doesn't work and the author of this book is just trying to sell snake oil, or c) god doesn't love you and you are unworthy of riches. But rarely does someone get curious and say, "Hmm . . . I see this process has worked for others, but didn't for me . . . Let me see what I can change to get better results!" This last response is rare. We have been taught and shaped culturally to expect immediate results. We want it, and we want it now. And we prefer to get it from someone who has already done it for us. Yes, we expect the person who has spent years and years studying, training, exploring, and experimenting to design us a simple system that will immediately turn us into magical wizards, easily and simply every single time. And we criticize them heavily if the system doesn't work for us or, god-forbid, the experts charge more than $9.95 for the simple system that they've designed after a decade or more of hard work!

Here is one of the very first paradoxes of the many you will encounter as you explore the world of consciousness: Creating your reality is easy and simple! It is! *And* you're going to have to apply yourself, as it can't be spoon-fed to you. Before you read further you should decide right now if you are one of those people who are looking for a quick fix. If so, I can tell you now, this book may disappoint you, for it requires you to practice. However, if you are the rarer type who is willing to question, experiment, play and explore with the concepts and ideas here, then please continue. You will soon embark on a fabulous journey of connecting more and more deeply to *all* of who you are. This is where you will find the power to create new possibilities. If you're unsure whether you are the latter type person, or if you think you're not but would really like to be, then I invite you to continue with me. You'll soon be learning about some tools that can help you easily move past the limitations you think you have!

When I first started playing with ideas of quantum creation, I was completely unsure that I could "do" it. You might recognize this doubt as something that will make you fail pretty quickly, if you are listening to most new age advice. Everyone claims that disbelief will limit you! You must completely believe to make it work! However I actually discovered that this wasn't true for me. My very first teachers who helped me explore these quantum fields were an intuitive healer named Stephan and his helper,

Wilson. I would spend the day with them in their Pioneer Square office, observing and learning. When a friend of mine sprained an ankle, even though I wasn't sure what I'd learned or what I was doing, I put my hands around the ankle in an attempt to heal it. Despite my disbelief that I could help, despite not knowing what I was doing, what do you know? The swelling went down in just a few moments! She also reported that as she rotated it, the pain was gone. Hmmm . . . curious! Yes, curious! Stay curious! This is the best advice for you whenever you play around with the manipulation of your reality, or the realities of others. And that goes double for the times when you seem to have had no effect at all on the reality you were trying to manipulate!

Since I had no idea what I did or how I did it, my success in healing seemed to indicate that knowing what or how was actually not necessary. But immediately, my little ego rebelled! *You need to know what you're doing! You need to be confident that you know how to fix people!* It raged on in my head. The ego needed to feel important. In the past it had felt important by "knowing" and by "knowing that it knew." I was smart, left-brained, a good student, and had always felt that I could understand pretty much anything as long as I spent enough time looking at the details, analyzing them, and seeing how they fit together. However, as much as I puzzled over the healing, I still could not figure out what had happened. The quantum theories and philosophies in use to explain these types of phenomena seemed to generate more questions than they answered.

Truthfully, our habitual ways of operating in the world will stop the majority of people in their tracks when facing something new and unknown. If the usual way of operating is not available to them, most people give up pretty darn quickly. I came across this inflexibility all the time in my career as an English instructor. A student would come to me and say, "Well I know that the paper was due yesterday, and that papers are not accepted late, but my car wouldn't start, so I couldn't make it to school." Let's think about this for a moment. Are cars the only mode of transportation available? No. The city has a nicely functioning bus system. The student's best friend, who lives down the street from him, made it to school that day, so a functioning mode of transportation must be available. And, if he perused the syllabus in a bit more detail, he might have discovered that emailing a digital version of the essay would suffice as presenting the work on time. Why would these solutions not occur to the student? I have no idea, really. Many of us have simply been taught to never think outside the box. If what we are used to doing doesn't work, we are completely limited and resigned to that outcome. We are masters of inventing lame excuses, but it does not occur to many of us to get curious and invent solutions.

This has, unfortunately, become the human condition: We are not creators or inventors. These designations are reserved for a very few unique "genius" types who then invent and create for us. The average person does not see herself as being inventive, and so the role of human has become extremely limited. If we are to exceed the old standards of human potential, if we want to move beyond these human limits, then it is time that we each step into a new role of creator/inventor. This means that we must get curious.

In fact, waiting around for me or anyone else to teach you

how to be inventive and creative is falling into the old mindset that you, yourself cannot come up with cool new solutions for your life. I want you to know that you can. You have everything you need inside of yourself! If you're not convinced, then by all means, read on. By the end of this book you will fully realize that YOU are all that you need to create an amazing new reality for your life.

FEELING INADEQUATE DOESN'T MATTER

Tip: Using Meta-Rule Sets

This very first tip that I am about to offer you has been by far the most effective tool in this game of expanding my awareness. I had so many limitations, you see, and if I wasn't careful, any one of these limitations could stop me on this path of conscious evolution that I so wanted to explore. This trick got me out of my own way, every time—no exceptions. I believe it can do the same for you, but remember to make this tool your own, to tweak and mold this concept until it fits you perfectly.

As I mentioned previously, my left brain was completely skeptical of the healing that was happening with my clients. So much so, that I used to think people were lying to me, just saying that they felt better because they felt sorry for me. I remember one friend, who had hurt her shoulder moving some heavy objects, asking me to perform some of these new energy healing techniques she'd heard me talking about. I was never sure what would happen, but I agreed. I used a few of the techniques I had learned, and then she moved her arm around and said, "Hey, thanks, that's much better!" Being the skeptic that I was, I asked, "How much better?" To which she replied, "About 70%!" She was clearly happy, and about to hop down from my table and run off, but I felt like a failure—only 70%! Why I must be a horrible healer if she didn't immediately improve 100%! "Wait," I said, and I made a few adjustments to the techniques. "Wow," she exclaimed. "That's fabulous!" And she hopped down and headed off to her next meeting. Of course, I sat there sure she was just putting me on, telling me she felt better so I wouldn't be humiliated! Isn't it funny how our low self-esteem can hold on tightly, even with direct evidence against it! But what was curious was that results happened, even though I wasn't convinced that they would. Results happened in spite of my disbelief.

How could this be? How did this healing work? I was not confident that I knew what I was doing! Uh-oh, right there is a limitation, and it is a strong enough limitation that it can potentially keep us from trying to play in these worlds of energy and consciousness. This is true no matter what methods or techniques we are learning. I would watch myself hesitate to offer help to my friends because I didn't know if this weird stuff would work or if my friends would just think I was weird! Then I'd realize that I was nervous and wasn't confident, and I'd hear in my head thoughts like *This isn't going to work.* I'd remember how my thoughts create results, as the gurus were all saying, and I'd despair thinking I just jinxed the healing. It really wouldn't work now, and on, and on. You can see what a vicious cycle this can be! It would be so easy to simply give up and not try to use my consciousness tools at all, the way my mind was spinning. I was getting in my own way! You can't win the lottery unless you buy a ticket. Similarly, you can't create new possibilities for yourself or others unless you give it a try.

This really wouldn't do. All of these thoughts swirling in my left brain, along with the feelings of uncertainty, were not helping me. While I had learned a rule from the Law of Attraction experts that my thoughts could create my reality, none of these thoughts were the reality that I wanted. So, as an experiment, I created a rule that superseded all other rules—a meta-rule. The word *meta* means transcending or more comprehensive. To use this concept of meta-rules, I would visualize a small circle around me that contained all the rules I operate on in my daily world. Then I would imagine another larger ring around the first circle. This larger ring would contain the meta-rules, and they would supersede any of the rules in the smaller circle.

My first meta-rule was exactly this: "No matter what my left brain thinks, it will not limit the results of my attempt to access change for this person." Notice I did not say that I would affect healing. I, for one, would never want to force healing onto people against their will. And even if their small will wanted to feel better, I had a belief that their higher will had a plan. Perhaps getting better wasn't the most useful thing for the individual. How would I know? I really did not want to do something energetically for a client and leave them worse than before. But since I didn't know what I was doing, how would I know?

It seems I had come up against another limiting belief that I might hurt someone. I didn't know much about medical issues when I was first starting out, and I had no idea if changing something for the person would simply make his condition worse. The thought of possibly hurting someone, was a very strong motivator to not try! So I created a second meta-rule for myself: "In my sessions with clients, either something more useful will occur for them, or nothing at all will happen." That eased my mind a great deal. I had limited "all possibilities which could occur" to a much narrower subset of "only more useful shifts." Alternatively, "nothing" could happen. At least that felt safe.

I remember one specific example when a client walked into my office. She had a number of different concerns and requests, one of which was to improve her eyesight. She had been experiencing the "normal" decline in eyesight that physicians tell us we should expect as we get older. My first thought when I heard her say she'd like her eyesight to improve was, *That's not possible!* I had a belief that eyesight was something difficult to affect for several reasons. I had heard others say this was a difficult task; when we are learning, it is easy to pick up other people's limitations. I had also attempted to change my own very poor eyesight and hadn't noticed much difference, so I was skeptical of the overall chance of this client's eyesight improving. However, even though I was completely sure that healing her eyesight wouldn't work, I remembered that I had a rule that whatever I heard in my head wouldn't affect the results, so I was willing to try.

Since I had no idea what to do, I used muscle testing. The rules of muscle testing are simple: The body knows if something is true or not. A muscle that you push on will stay strong when the statement is true, and become weak if the statement is untrue. I used the statement: I have a strategy. And the answer was an immediate "yes!" Well, since I had no idea what this strategy was, I just proceeded with the first idea that popped into my head and what do you know! She exclaimed suddenly, "Oh wait! That's much better! I can see things more sharply now, and it's just a little blurry in one eye." I continued the session, and sure enough, she added, "Oh there we go! The blurriness went away. That's great!" She left clearly happy but I shook my head, still in disbelief. I was sure that if it worked, it was only because she was an unusual woman, already well-steeped in the weird world of consciousness. *It wouldn't work on an ordinary person*, I told myself.

Later that night, however, I had a moment of understanding as I slipped off to sleep, seeing how such a shift could occur. By the time I awoke the next day, I had forgotten what the insight was. But in the original moment of understanding, I had tweaked my own eyesight pattern. The next week I went to the eye doctor, and my very poor eyesight had improved an entire point! I remember keeping both the old and the new numbers on my prescription posted on my bulletin board for some time, as evidence that changes can happen, even for someone as ordinary as myself! What was truly amazing, now that I look back on these experiences, is that the simple concept of creating a meta-rule prevented me from giving up. And because I tried, results happened. Over time, I was able to build up a nice list of successful examples of results, thus creating the evidence my left brain needed to feel more confidence. Even if I didn't know what I was doing, at least it was working!

While these stories are great examples of success, we need to be okay with nothing happening at times. Many of us want to see something happen every time because this is good for the ego; it grows confidence. But the downside to having a rule that something must happen every time, is that you may encounter clients who are already in the best place they can be. In such cases, even a small change could possibly leave them worse than when they arrived. I was willing to compromise my ego gratification for the safety and best possible outcome for my clients, hard as it was! If you use these tools only for yourself and your family, then you will be very motivated to avoid making a situation worse. The meta-rule—"either something more useful will occur, or nothing at all will happen"—means sometimes, nothing will happen.

What takes some getting used to is the idea that experiencing pain or sickness could possibly be the best outcome for you or a client, while healing might not be. It is a tricky place to stand. We believe that we want to have control over our own realities—have completely healthy bodies that are young and vibrant; have fulfilling, deep, intimate, and satisfying relationships; and have fully abundant and resourced bank accounts—so we can pursue whatever our passion is without being restricted in any way. Yes! If we were able to create our realities, then of course we would choose to have no pain, suffering, or challenges, right? As I examined this impulse in myself, it seemed to come mostly from my ego. I want a beautifully smooth life where everything goes my way. I want to be happy all the time! I want everyone to agree with me! I want a partner who is gorgeous, whom I admire and look up to, and who treats me like a princess! I want so much money that I never have to work and I can pursue my bliss!

However when I look at such a life, I think in the end it

would be very boring. No challenges? Nothing left to learn? Just a pursuit and indulgence of every last whim and desire endlessly? Fun for awhile, but then what? Well, that seems a little like the desires of a two-year-old. Oh yes, humans are such toddlers in the realm of spirit. On the one hand I want to honor this ego, because it brings so many of us into these pursuits of expanding and evolving—wanting to heal myself, wanting to get my perfect life—and yes for sure, some of that is going to happen! But as we move further along in this expansion, we realize that letting go of such ego driven pursuits is where the real magic lies! And so, love the ego part of you that has brought you here, and be willing to move beyond it. Be willing to let go of your quest for perfection, as that is the only way to be truly perfect! Letting go of the need to control marks the beginning of expansion into limitlessness.

Every time I came up against a limitation that threatened to keep me from moving forward in my practice of consciousness explorations, including the healing work I was doing professionally, I simply made up a new meta-rule. Having a meta-rule in place freed me up to move forward, despite my concerns and doubts. The beauty of meta-rules is that I did not have to change myself. I could be my imperfect self, worried and uncertain, and I was still able to achieve results with my clients.

Meta-rules are such a crucial concept, that I encourage you to set up your own system however you need it to work for you. You cannot wait to cure yourself of all your issues, limitations, and problems, before you move forward and allow yourself the expansion that you are looking for. This system of using meta-rules can bypass many years of effort. And as you'll see as you continue reading, the issues with self-esteem and confidence and negative thinking, simply begin to dissolve when you don't put any energy into them.

At this point someone always asks me, "How did you make your rules? Did you write them down?" Well this is exactly the piece that you are going to want to explore for yourself. Do you need to write a calligraphy sign with the rules and post it in your office? Is just deciding on the rule enough? Play around and see what works for you, as there is no right or wrong way to make up a rule. The exercise included here can help you decide what meta-rules you'd like to create, and I've added a few examples to get you started.

EXERCISE

Creating Your Meta-Rules

1. Generate a list of all the reasons why you think you can't create your own reality with consciousness or energy tools:

   a) People will think I'm weird.

   b) I might hurt someone.

   c) It probably won't work.

   d) _____

   e) _____

   f) _____

2. Create your corresponding rule. Use something really easy, like "it doesn't matter," to start these rules:

a) It doesn't matter what the other person thinks, it won't influence the results of the session.

b) The results will be more useful or nothing at all will happen.

c) It doesn't matter what negative thought I have in my head, it can't limit the results of the session.

d) _____

e) _____

f) _____

THE LIMITATIONS OF MIND

I grew up valuing brain power. This is not unusual in western society. Most of us keep our conscious awareness in our head. Unfortunately that's the least useful place for it to be if we're going to navigate well in consciousness and create new possibilities for ourselves. The awareness we are looking for isn't centered in our brains at all. But moving our awareness anywhere else can really cause problems for many people. What I've noticed is that many, many of us want to believe in magic, want to believe that we could be clairvoyant, want to believe that there is something other than the 3-D world we've been stuck with. But we are terrified of seeming crazy to others—to spouses, friends, parents, etc. If we begin to "see" things, for example, how can we be certain that what we are seeing is real. What if we're just imagining it?

This classic dilemma definitely occurred for me on my path. I had always valued my intelligence and ability to think logically. While I wanted magic in my life, I felt I needed evidence. However most things surrounding consciousness and reality creation are fraught with paradoxes, and this was no exception. The paradox is this: if you don't believe until you see, you will never see the magic. Only by believing it's possible, and beginning to notice the magic, can you see more and more of it. If you don't believe it is there, then you never see it. This will confirm your own suspicion that there is no evidence and thus create a reality without any magic. Ahhh! It's a logic lover's nightmare! But even for those who are skeptics—and I was definitely a skeptic when I started—there is hope. Remember to use your meta-rules. A good one for you if you have a lot of disbelief is: "It doesn't matter whether I believe in it or not, it won't limit my results."

Tip: Learning to Move Your Consciousness

A second way to cure the problem of mind is to expand your consciousness by moving it out of your head. If you're in your head, you will have the least ability to notice where the magic is. Once you are able to move your conscious awareness out of your head, you are more likely to notice all the cool stuff! A logical person checks into their head to see if they're noticing anything unusual. As I mentioned previously, you'll want to get used to doing the opposite. Get outside of the brain game and you'll become aware of so much more!

One friend of mine who was in this skeptical, brainy state of mind, told me that he always seems to have friends like me, who can traverse all these amazing realms of consciousness. But he has never experienced anything magical himself and so he has to wonder. He said to me, "I think maybe when you were a little girl, you loved unicorns so much, you began to see them." What he was saying is that because he hasn't had an experience, he believes these worlds are made up! And that's a very logical conclusion. But when you realize that the world you are used to accepting as real is made up too, then you have a little more slippage into the other worlds. Are they made up? Yes, they are as made up as the 3-D illusion you now believe is reality.

I begin many of my introductory classes and workshops by saying just that. Our current 3-D reality is an illusion as much as it is real. Any other reality that we create is equally an illusion and equally real. Why would we bother to change and shift our reality then? Well, why wouldn't we want to shift into a reality that is more useful, or brings us more joy, or allows us to have more fun? My best advice is to always choose to go where your excitement and fun lie. If you find fun and excitement in the everyday consensual mainstream reality, then you don't need to explore in this way. But if you find that the current reality is not fun for you, then you can develop the skills and abilities to create a more useful one.

The next chapter will offer some basic tools to begin shifting your conscious awareness out of your head and into the spaces where you can begin to notice the magic. And this is key! Don't skip over learning this part. Without this one ability, additional techniques and tools will be of limited use. But with this one ability, so much more becomes possible.

2

THE BASICS OF EXPANDING CONSCIOUSNESS

BEGIN WHERE YOU CAN BEGIN

There is always more than one route to the outcome you are seeking. However, to keep it simple, we will only explore a couple of starting points here. To allow your mind access to "other worlds," you might find it useful to have your left brain agree that experiencing unseen worlds is a possibility, a possibility that even you can have access to.

Start from the premise that there is evidence—scientific evidence even—that energies are present that you cannot see or feel or smell. We cannot see microwaves or infrared waves, but we know they exist because we have devices that can measure them. Much of the universe exists in this unseen form. Scientists estimate that 90% of the universe is "dark matter"—something that is beyond our abilities to see or even measure. The human senses can only calibrate information from a very small range of frequencies. Furthermore, of the impulses that our senses can calibrate, only a small fraction of these make it into our brain for interpretation. Much of what we are accessing right now with our senses is being filtered. Are you aware, in this moment, of your little toe on your left foot? Were you aware of it before I mentioned it? We are filtering multitudes of sensory input every second and ignoring much of what is there.

Magnitudes of information exist in frequency ranges that are beyond our ability to sense with the sensory organs of the physical body. And yet, people regularly report having access to this information. We've all come into contact with someone who has what we term as "extra-sensory" perception. Whether it is a mother's intuition that her child needs her even though they are miles apart or grandma's premonitions that always came true, most of us know someone who has the strange ability to access information beyond their five senses. If you can accept that there are frequencies that our regular senses can't pick up, and you see that others have access to some of this, then clearly the possibility exists that even you can tap into these other worlds!

Another angle you may want to consider as a way to appease your left brain is to delve into the leading quantum theories of prominent physicists. When these physicists examined very, very small subatomic particles, they realized that there is a certain point where matter coheres. Before this point, it does not exist in physical form. Indeed, much speculation has been made of this pre-matter phase being composed of simply a field of probabilities. This means that the information exists prior to becoming matter as not just pure potential, but as multiple pure potentials. The information is out there even if it is not in a physical form.

Now consider who you are as consciousness. Are you limited to your physical body? Most people who are familiar with the power of their thoughts or their dreams would likely agree that they are more than their physical body. The Monroe Institute is a great resource for people who would like to explore themselves beyond their physical bodies. In terms of awareness, I would suggest that human consciousness can become aware of itself on many levels outside of our physical 3-D experience. All that is required is tuning our awareness to the place just beyond the point where information and potential cohere into matter. This type of tuning explains why there are people who have premonitions that come true. Perhaps you think of a friend who calls you minutes later. You may already be picking up the thoughts and feelings of those around you, which are simply information that has not cohered into matter or experience yet.

If your left brain can concede one or more of these points— that energies exist that cannot be measured by our physical senses; that beyond matter, potentials of possibility exist as patterns of light and information; that some people can pick up on these energies and patterns—then you have enough flexibility in your consciousness right now to start experiencing these phenomena yourself.

FIND JOY FIRST

You may have picked up this book hoping you would get a three-step lesson on how to manifest, with your thought alone, money in your bank account instantly. Or perhaps you want to heal your physical body without allopathic intervention. There are many ways you can affect the 3-D reality you experience every day, once you have tapped into these other worlds that I am mentioning. My experience, however, is that it takes some time to create enough momentum in these worlds to be truly effective in orchestrating the changes you desire. Just start where you can start. Be curious, persistent, and explore, explore, explore—for the sheer fun of it! Let go right now of some of the goals and outcomes you are hoping to achieve and you will find you progress much more quickly. The sheer joy of exploration will take you much farther than focusing on "fixing" a problem you are experiencing. I understand that this approach can seem easier said than done, as our ego's desires can assert a lot of pressure at times. Regardless, I hope you proceed with the excitement of discovery as your guide.

One of your goals should be to move easily through "spaces" of consciousness, at will and fluently. Most of us keep our awareness focused on the usual: what we are doing in the 3-D world right now, or what happened in the past that we are emotionally attached to, or what will happen tomorrow if we don't come up with the rent money. However, to be fluent in consciousness, fluent enough to create leverage in our 3-D life, we need to spend more time in some of the atypical spaces of consciousness. The exercises in this chapter will help you begin this exploration. Ideally, you should become fluent in each before moving on.

GATHERING YOURSELF TO BEGIN

In daily life our consciousness exists in a fairly spread out form. Most of us are thinking of the tasks we need to accomplish throughout the day, going over the contents of conversations and events that happened early in the week, and maybe even projecting ahead to a welcome vacation that will occur the following month. We spread out our consciousness over time, a habit that keeps us from accessing powerful spaces that offer us the leverage we desire in creating our reality.

This seemingly small task of being able to gather yourself will become hugely useful to you in many ways. When you hear people talking about being present, this is what they mean. "Present" means *all* of you is here right now in this moment. You may have heard about how the *now* is a place you need to have access to in order to tap into the power of possibilities. Indeed, I agree that this is an important key to creating new possibilities, along with having a solid knowing of who you are. By being connected to who you are and by being completely present in the moment, you will have access to much leverage when it comes to creation.

Many healing techniques or systems for manifestation do not discuss the importance of being present. Why is this concept left out? Because it is practically impossible to teach! Connecting with yourself in this moment is really beyond words and tools. It's much easier to advise you to watch your thoughts and to create affirmations. But, in my experience, it's not what you think that is most important, it is *where* you think it from.

The *where* I am referring to is a most powerful place for

transformation—heart-space. Gathering yourself into the present will allow you to access heart-space. The exercises we'll use will help you explore in the direction you need to go. But you will need to always look inside yourself to judge whether your path needs some tweaks, turns or rotations in order to connect with your authentic self. It is not something anyone else can do for you.

Oh no, you worry that now I'm going to tell you that you have to meditate in stillness for long periods! Like you have time for that, right? Well you're in luck. While you will need to practice bringing your awareness into one central place, it's something that can be done anytime, anywhere. Indeed, you will want to restructure your thinking about time and about how to be in the world, so that you are operating from this place of power all the time, quite naturally.

But now, while you are relaxed, let's experiment a little.

First, think back over the day briefly. And then think about tomorrow's day. Notice where your awareness goes while you are thinking about these things. By awareness, I do not mean thoughts. This is the first distinction you will need to make. Awareness is not thought; it is a listening from within. To notice your awareness, you actually need to get out of your head. Uh-oh, another sticking point for so many of us thinkers. How do you get your awareness out of your head? The exercises in this chapter will help. This one very crucial ability is not negotiable in learning to navigate consciousness. You will need to dedicate much time with this important first ability, because once you can get out of your head, everything else will flow. Without this ability, you will struggle with the rest of the exercises.

❖

EXERCISE

Gathering Yourself

It's easy to collect this awareness that you've spread out throughout the day.

• Spread out your hands. This represents all of where your consciousness is. Feel your awareness in this spread-out state.

• Slowly bring your hands together. Notice softly how this changes the *where* of your awareness.

• Put your hands up next to your eyes, as if you're wearing the kind of blinders horses wear to cut off their peripheral vision.

• Slowly move your hands out laterally from your head, and then back in. Notice how your awareness can expand and contract to fill the space between your hands.

• Try it with your eyes open, then closed.

• Try any other variations you can think of, to notice and gather your awareness back into a central place. Usually that central place is the physical body—it's a pretty easy marker to use!

Practice this throughout the day. The more times you practice, the easier other more advanced exercises will be. Don't forget to play and explore. Be curious about anything that shows up for you during this exercise. If you hear your mind judging how you're doing, send your mind into the other room to play while you try this out.

GETTING OUT OF YOUR HEAD

Once you have some practice gathering yourself and being able to sit with all of your awareness in the present moment, you will want to experiment with taking that focused awareness and moving it consciously to various "locations" at will. The heart is the center of expanded awareness. There are many books talking about the heart field, how to live and think there. The field of the heart provides us with a very strong link to the aspects of ourselves beyond our 3-d human form. It can also tap us into a field of possibilities that we can explore and use as we create.

The heart, then, is a really good place to begin when trying to move your consciousness out of your head. You have a pretty clear idea about where this location is, given that you know where your physical heart is; the energetic heart field is near the actual physical heart. So ask yourself, how can you go about this task of moving your awareness down from your head to your heart? How many options or techniques can you think of? I'll share a few, but there are likely to be hundreds. The best one for you may not be the ones I discuss. But use this information as a guide, pointing you in the direction that you would like to go. As always, your path may be very unique to you!

❖

EXERCISE

Moving into Your Heart-Space

• Start with your eyes closed. We are so visually biased that it can be difficult to separate our consciousness from being behind our eyes. Later you can try the same techniques with your eyes open.

• Remember the trick where you used your hands to expand and compress your awareness? Use your hands again. This time put them in front of your eyes, palms down. Center your awareness just under the hands and slowly move your hands down to just above your heart. You should notice that your awareness goes with your hands.

• Or, imagine your awareness as a miniature you sitting in your head behind your eyes. Have this miniature you move to the back of your head and climb down a ladder placed against your spine until it reaches your heart.

• Focus on your breathing. Take big breaths in and out. Imagine that the in-breaths and out-breaths are coming in and out through the heart field, instead of entering and leaving the body through the nose.

• Vocalize a tone or *om* sound. Focus your awareness on the vibration that sound makes in your chest area.

Practice any time you are just hanging out doing nothing, waiting in line, during a commercial, or while sitting at a red light or stop sign. Build this exercise into your daily life until you can drop into your heart at will, quickly and easily.

Do not move on to the following exercises until you can do this one fluently. This is one area where you want a solid foundation.

ADVANCED AWARENESS EXERCISES

Once you have gotten the hang of moving your awareness into your heart, you will want to explore moving it beyond the physical body. In many ways, you do this automatically and naturally—in dreams and daydreaming moments, for example. For our purposes, you will need to learn how to experience this movement willfully and at your direction.

So take a moment and relax, closing your eyes. Think back to the previous instructions of gathering yourself. The first instruction says to allow your awareness to think back over the day. When you do this, notice where your awareness goes. If you can't tell, focus on where your eyes move even though your eyes are closed. Do they move towards the left? Towards the right? Do they seem to sink in? Roll up? This is one clue to where you have mapped the awareness of your immediate past.

Your answers are unique to you. Although many of us tend to have similar mappings, there is no right answer to where the immediate past should be located in your awareness. In the next chapter, we will discuss mapping in depth. But for now, just notice that when you think of a past time, your awareness moves to a place that is typically not in your body at all. I've included here two exercises I used to help me gain the ability to move my awareness at will.

These exercises use a system of organization that has been around a long time. You already know that we humans have a physical body, and you may also have heard of the emotional body. Furthermore we also have mental and spiritual bodies. The term "bodies" really means that there are fields where emotional, mental, and spiritual information exist.

Let's imagine that each of these fields of information exist as a layer of energy, or a field around the physical body. In truth, a better description would be that these fields overlap and permeate the physical body, but imagining them as distinct is perfectly fine for our purposes. This exercise has no goal other than to explore what each of these bodies feel like to you. You may be surprised about what you notice. Some of you may find it difficult to notice much about one or more of these bodies. If that's the case, don't worry. With practice, these exercises will expand your ability to experience all of these realms.

EXERCISE

Moving through Your Bodies

- Relax and take a few deep breaths.

- Start by using the "Gathering Yourself" practice.

- Once you are relaxed and present, center your awareness within your physical body.

- Notice where it feels tight, warm, cool, or tingly.

- Just observe any sensations you notice without trying to change them.

- Now imagine that there is an energetic layer or field surrounding your body like a nested doll. We will call this your emotional body.

- Allow your awareness to expand out from your physical body and into this emotional field.

- Observe closely. Where does your awareness want to go? For example, I might notice that I am drawn to the place in this field that lies above my abdominal area.

- Give yourself as much time as you like to wander your awareness around this field. Notice where your attention sticks, and where it moves past quickly.

- Now, imagine a layer of the nested doll surrounding the emotional body. We will call this the mental body.

- Expand your awareness into this space and notice as you have been.

- Finally, imagine another nested doll energy field beyond the mental body. We will call this the spiritual body.

- Expand your awareness into the spiritual body and notice as you have been.

- Practice this exercise daily for a week and observe what changes you notice over time.

❖ ❖ ❖

❖

EXERCISE

Moving Up and Down

In this exercise, imagine a tube above your head that runs through your body and into the earth. Some people believe that our "higher" selves are above our physical body, while our "lower" or "shadow" selves are buried and hidden below the physical body. This spatial arrangement is merely a conceptual tool. Such an organization does not apply to the next exercise, which is simply an exercise to help you expand past your current awareness limits.

• Start with your awareness centered in your physical body.

• Allow your awareness to move up through your body and out the top of your head, yet still contained within this tube.

• How far above the head can your awareness get? Perhaps you can't move above your head at all. Perhaps you can move a foot or so above. No matter how far, just make a note of it.

• Now bring your awareness back to your physical center.

• Allow your awareness to move down through your body and out through your feet, yet still contained within this tube.

• How far below your feet can you move your awareness? Again, no matter how far, just make a note of it.

• Now repeat this exercise daily for a week or two, and see how these distances expand. Much like doing push-ups, your ability increases with practice.

DISCOVERING THE BIG YOU

Tip: You Are Not Your Thoughts

When I was a beginner exploring these spaces beyond my physical body, I recognized that getting out of my head was going to be a crucial aspect for success. However, I was a very left-brained person! I had a difficult time moving my awareness anywhere at all. The first time I tried to move my awareness into my heart, I felt that I couldn't get it far from my head at all. I was very mentally focused. Having been an excellent student all of my life, I had wrapped my identity tightly around the idea that I was intelligent. I used my mental abilities to create a sense of control in my world. I could use logic and reason to produce fairly good results when it came to creating a life.

However, by allowing myself to get so attached to my thoughts and my intellectual abilities, I was limiting my ability to experience the world in some pretty important ways. For example, when I first started doing healing work, I would hear many negative thoughts in my head: *The client is going to think I'm new-agey and ditzy because I can't explain what I am doing. This person is probably more intuitive than me, and so he is going to realize I'm a fraud and I'm just pretending to do something as I wave my hands around!* Because I was so attached to my mental life, these unfortunate thoughts created my experience. I began to feel hesitant and afraid. My confidence and self-esteem would vanish because the negative thoughts were, in effect, the most powerful force shaping things for me at that time. I would hear the thought: *You're not good enough!* And immediately, I would have an emotional reaction, feeling sad, negative, or depressed. These thoughts were so loud, I believed that surely they were true. Looking back now, I can remember how powerful thoughts were in my world.

Others might tell you that you need to banish these negative thoughts and replace them with positive affirmations, in effect changing your thoughts to have a more positive experience. However this allows us to continue believing that our thoughts are who we are and that they are important creators of our reality. As you learn about manifestation techniques from people in the field, you are likely to hear that thoughts create your reality. This is both true and not true. It is true if you are identified with your thoughts. If you experience emotional reactions in relation to your thoughts, then your thoughts will very much color your experience. However, you can also emerge into a larger awareness where you notice that you are not your thoughts! Your thoughts simply are a synaptic firing of some brain cells, and you are so much more than that! Once you find that you no longer believe that your thoughts are who you are, you will experience a profound freedom. This has been the most profound lesson I have learned to date, but I did not accomplish it using positive affirmations.

Instead, my secret was to use my meta-rule sets. As I discussed earlier, I would invoke a meta-rule that would supersede the thoughts I was having. My most useful rule was this: No matter what I am thinking, my thoughts cannot affect the results of the session. I used this one frequently because I had heard that if I had a negative thought such as "This isn't going to work," then I would end up creating that reality! So I just made a rule that would trump the thought and make it ineffective. I did not waste my time trying to eliminate all my negative thoughts! I like to claim that this is because I'm rather lazy. I really did not have the time or inclination to fix all my failings in order to become a powerful healer. I wanted to take the quickest road that I could—an impulse that can backfire at times, but in this case, an amazing thing happened!

As I implemented this meta-rule, that it did not matter what I thought or felt, a funny thing happened. I began to realize that the thinking *I* was not important in this alchemical formula of healing. The small *I*, the ego—who wanted to "do" something for others, who wanted to feel accomplished as a healer, who wanted to have an identity as a great healer in these realms of magic and energy—that *I* didn't matter at all! The results occurred despite my thoughts. The thoughts that used to feel important, that I identified as *me*, really didn't matter. It was a huge blow to my ego, but it was hugely freeing at the same time!

Tip: Gaining Leverage with Your Emotions

Once I realized that my thoughts were not really me, I began to suspect that my emotions weren't really me either. Perhaps emotions were just another ego experience of the small self. So I began to experiment. We all know that when we are feeling a powerful emotion, it is very hard to imagine not feeling it. Emotions have a magnetic quality that draws our awareness into them. We can be drawn into a negative emotion so completely and inexplicably that we can get caught in it for a very long time. Positive feelings, however, like joy and excitement, seem to fade more easily. We rarely become trapped in them as we do with the negative emotions.

When considering ways of thinking about emotional energy, it occurred to me that if I could create a model that my mind could understand, it would be easier to shift the negative emotions. I wouldn't say that the model I settled on is actually what is happening when we experience strong emotions, but the concepts helped me shift to a more useful place. If these ideas help you, fantastic! If not, don't get stuck in an inability to shift emotions when you need to. Instead, get curious and find out what will work for you. For me, the model that worked best was an electromagnetic model to understand the vortex I can get trapped in when experiencing strong emotions.

Thoughts appear to me to have electrical properties. This makes sense, as our brains fire electrically when we produce thoughts. But thoughts alone, or electrical impulses alone, don't seem to have a big impact on reality (as I discussed in the previous section, "You Are Not Your Thoughts.") On the other hand, emotions seem to be magnetic in nature, drawing our awareness to them fairly consistently. When a thought (electrical) is hooked up with an emotion (magnetic) then we have a tangle of electromagnetism. Not all thoughts are tagged with emotions, but the ones that are seem to have the ability to self-perpetuate. Long after a trauma happens, if we think of the situation, we get drawn back into the powerful emotions as well. We can replay these patterns over and over. What's worse, this type of electro-magnetic distortion seems to attract other similar distortions that will strengthen it. This idea, then, can explain the popular belief that like attracts like. We do attract similar vibrations to us when we are experiencing these destructive patterns. This is one area where I do see validity in the Law of Attraction theory, as I've observed and experienced it.

I don't believe that experiencing negative or painful emotions is bad for us generally. In fact, it is part of the human experience. In truth, without these "negative" emotions, we would be unable to experience happiness. Without the contrast, the experience of happiness would not really make sense in a dualistic 3-D experience. But whenever we become caught in a replaying vortex of pain, then we can take action to dissipate the energy gathering within it. Having a set of tools in no way means that you won't experience unhappiness, but it can provide a way to shift the pattern, and begin to feel better more quickly. Being lazy, my favorite tool is simple: dispersing the vortex with pure consciousness.

How can pure consciousness make a shift like this? Again consider the idea of how electro-magnetic forces work. Molecules often have a positive or a negative end, and that slight charge creates an attraction to the oppositely charged ends of other molecules. In chemistry, if you want to separate molecules, you do so by increasing the energy to break the bond. Since pure consciousness is energy, you are untangling the pattern in a similar manner to breaking a molecular bond.

Often, once the pattern is disrupted, it doesn't return in its original state. It may return, but will generally be quite different from the original pattern. Once you have practiced the next exercise, you may need only one attempt to completely and permanently shift your pattern. But if you need to repeat it, don't despair. You have the tool to shift it again. Each time you do it, you are participating in the magic of consciousness. Does it really matter how many times you repeat it, as long as you achieve your desired result in the end? Get excited about any result you obtain and you'll see the results expand exponentially!

EXERCISE

Dispersing the Emotional Vortex

This exercise should be used when you are having an experience of strong negative emotion. However, you can practice it by thinking about an issue that normally upsets you. Let the feelings arise and then try out the following instructions:

- Once you are feeling the strong emotion, notice where in or around your body you are experiencing it.

- The quickest way to disperse this tangle of energy is to "push" your awareness through it. This means move your consciousness through the pattern and out the other side. When pure consciousness interacts with the pattern, it often dissipates significantly.

- If you find that some of the pattern still exists, you can repeat the exercise.

The feeling I have after dispersing an unhappy or painful emotion is one of simple neutrality. I can think of the issue that initiated the emotion and stay calm and neutral. At times it may seem impossible to feel good when we are really upset or sad. However, practicing bringing ourselves to neutral, is an important skill. You really want to have this one in your tool kit.

In the second half of this book, I will share ways to create and shift your reality into something that is more fun and useful for you. As you practice, you will notice that being neutral is an important key for shifting the patterns that are making up your reality. It's a cruel paradox that the more emotionally invested you are in a specific outcome, the less leverage you will have over creating the shifts that you want. If you find yourself emotionally caught up in an expected outcome, separating from the emotion and becoming neutral can be enough to give you leverage over your reality. Practicing getting to a neutral place when you notice you are trapped in a negative emotion is a good place to start.

The "Dispersing the Emotional Vortex" exercise will help you practice becoming neutral, but there are many other tools that work well. Many people find that the Emotional Freedom Technique (EFT) tapping works remarkably well for them. If you haven't tried EFT tapping, this is another great option; I've seen many people benefit from it. A quick internet search will give you some of the EFT basic tools to get started. As you continue through the book, you'll find many other tools that will help you build on this.

Once you find a tool to bring an emotion to neutral, the second component is cultivating the positive feelings and emotions. The more you practice being happy, the more your body just naturally *is* happy. As you move through the book, you'll find exercises that will help you practice happiness as well.

3

MAPPING THE TERRITORY OF CONSCIOUSNESS

BASIC MAPS

One of the challenges when I began my explorations in consciousness was that I felt I needed someone to guide me, so I'd get it right. This was unknown territory for me, a blank map. I thought I needed to "go" somewhere. I wondered about which direction and how to get there. I did not yet understand that spaces in consciousness were not places "out there" somewhere. Rather, this was an internal exploration.

However, as I began to explore I noticed something: Everyone does things slightly differently! When someone else shows you how to explore consciousness, what they are really showing you is their personal map. Some maps belong to a group. For example a shamanic map will be taught to shamanic practitioners, who will follow that map with great results. Practitioners of another modality will be taught another map, and that map will give them great results for what they are doing. All maps are real and all provide great results in their specific areas. If you come across something in one map that you'd rather not be involved with, then you can simply exit the map you are in and use a different one!

Because we come to consciousness from a 3-D world, we are used to having structure. Structures are useful as we begin, but will eventually be limiting. As consciousness evolves, it becomes more fluid and changeable. It is useful to remember that no structure, concept, or map will be able to accurately depict "Truth" or "Reality" of consciousness. Usually, the best we can do in the beginning is to trade one limiting structure for a less limiting structure. This is a great place to start!

FINDING THE PRESENT NOW

Let's start with the activity where you gather yourself from the day and get all of yourself present in the moment. In the 3-D world we have the structure of past, present, and future. Most people spend the most time in the past or the future—thinking about issues that have bothered them in the past, or worrying about what is going to happen in the future. However, the present—the "now" moment—is the place where you lose yourself in a world that is beyond thought. It's the "chop wood, carry water" place of no thought. Try the exercise "Discovering the Space Between" to find that present "now."

EXERCISE

Discovering the Space Between

• Decide on a word to be your mantra, such as "peace" or "one."

• Begin to repeat this word in your mind.

• Notice that there is a space between these word-thoughts.

• Place your awareness on this space between. If this seems difficult, then imagine that the space between the words contains a light.

• Move your awareness into the space or into the light.

• Observe that space getting larger, or the light getting brighter, as you move your awareness into it.

• Notice that when you move into the space, your eyes soften focus. You may feel more aware of and present in your heart. You are in a space without thoughts directing you. You are in space where you are able to more directly access *who you really are*.

• Once you move into this space, ask in your mind to amplify this feeling . . . twice, ten times, 1,000 times.

This is a state you want to practice accessing every day. By doing so, you will create easy access to the space of consciousness that you need to get real effects in shaping your world. When I first started, I would practice every day, every time I had a free moment—waiting in line at the bank, washing dishes, during commercials. Being present is the single most important activity that I can recommend for expanding your consciousness and accessing more of who you really are.

Exploring from the Present

Once you are in the present *now* moment, you are in a position to have more leverage in your world. Since everything is accessible from the *now*, this is always where you want to begin. The reason why affirmations often don't create the outcomes we expect is because two requirements are missing: 1) the *now* moment, which is a *place* in consciousness that we create from and 2) the heart-space, which is a *space* of awareness that we create from.

The place of now and the space of heart are inextricably linked, existing together to create a powerful point of transformation. Thinking thoughts from a normal waking state, or beta brainwave state, will not manifest much. While you can work with changing brainwaves in order to find this point of transformation, all you really need is simply to be out of your head. Being *in your head,* or thinking from a normal state of consciousness, is not where the power is.

In addition to the "Discovering the Space Between" exercise, many other exercises in this book will help you practice accessing this state that gets you out of your head. Refer to Appendix A if you want to quickly find related exercises.

What's the Catch?

One of the "catches" and ironies to this process is that in the now-place/heart-space of transformation, one does not really think. So how then do you manifest the things you want when there is no way of focusing your intention? Although there are many ritual magic techniques to do just that, I recommend simply being in the *now*. There really is nothing else to do. The more you exist in the *now*, the more your awareness expands, and creating flows naturally. No need to force it. No need to *try* anything. After existing in this space of transformation for a while, you will notice that the world responds to you quite naturally.

For example, one day, after I had been moving in this heart-space vibration for several weeks, I had a thought that a cup of tea would be lovely. I walked into the kitchen and strangely, the tea was sitting there steaming, already made! A small part of me wondered if I just had a senior moment. Maybe I had come into the kitchen earlier and made the tea, and simply forgot. Could that have possibly happened? Perhaps. But by this stage in my consciousness explorations, I was willing to accept that magical things do happen, and reality can show up in these seamless ways. Accepting grace and magic as it moves in your life is a key to experiencing more and more of it. I celebrated this phenomenon as an indication that I had successfully invited grace and magic into my reality.

From Present to Where?

As beginners we may wonder, if my consciousness is going to expand, where will it expand to? That depends on you. Since anything you can think of already exists, you might want to explore some very basic maps first.

Let's try a very basic shamanic map that is broken into three main "spaces": the lower, middle, and upper worlds. In a basic shamanic map, the middle world is the world you live in. It can also represent the present time. Being aware of a person just moments before she calls you is an example of gathering information from the middle world. The lower world is a realm that can represent the unconscious. It can also represent the past. You can gain information from the past in the lower world. You can also make changes to past events and heal old wounds. The upper world is a realm that can represent archetypes, gods, and spirits. Creating and manifesting can happen here. Visit one of these worlds in the "Visiting the Lower World" exercise.

EXERCISE

Visiting the Lower World

- Close your eyes and relax. Go into the space between your thoughts . . . when you are in the *now,* relax and wait . . . amplify the feeling if you like.

- Notice that you are sitting on some very comfortable earth, under a tree near a meadow. Feel and experience the sounds, smells and sights.

- You will eventually find yourself drawn in a specific direction.

- Move in that direction until you come to an opening in

the earth. It might look like stairs down into a cave, or just a mossy opening through some bushes. This is the entrance to the lower world. Don't get caught up in the description. You can simply follow a road that goes downhill, for example. However you access the lower world is the right way.

- When you enter, look around and explore.

- Eventually you will be approached by a guide. The guide may look human or be in the form of an animal.

- Ask the guide about anything you'd like to know . . . about a problem you have or a physical illness you are experiencing.

- The guide will communicate, talk to you or show you places in the lower world that will bring you answers.

- Follow the guide and ask for clarification when you need it. Ask for instructions on how to change the problem. The answers are often simple: bathe in a pond there or turn and walk north. The guide will let you know.

- The guide may have a gift for you. Ask if there is anything you need to leave behind with the guide.

- You may leave thoughts, beliefs, patterns, etc. . . . whatever is not useful to you anymore.

- When it is time to go, the guide will lead you back to the portal through which you entered.

- Slowly find your way back to the comfortable earth, under the tree, near the meadow.

• Wiggle your fingers and toes as you integrate the changes into your physical body.

• Some people say their name as they open their eyes to represent their re-emergence into the middle world.

Further explore the lower and upper worlds. Typically, as the name suggests, you move into the lower world through an opening in the ground. To move into the upper world you go up: through an opening in the clouds, for example, or taking an escalator up through the clouds. Again, however it appears to you is fine. In all cases there are guides to escort you.

You can draw maps of your explorations. The basic map would have the lower world on the bottom third of the paper, the upper world on the top third, and the middle world in the middle. Your detailed map of your lower, upper, and middle worlds will be unique to you.

OTHER MAPS FOR UNSEEN WORLDS

There are many, many maps that you can explore. I highly recommend the book, *Ascension Magic*, by Christopher Penczak. He outlines a number of maps and shows the correlations between maps. Some examples of possible maps to explore are:

• The Tree of Life—a ladder representing levels of consciousness. Seekers begin with Malkuth, the sphere of the physical world, and then explore the other spheres.

- Seven Planes of Existence: Physical, Etheric, Astral, Emotional, Mental, Psychic, Divine. (Other maps may list more than seven and/or the names may be different.)
- Dimensions of Light—often arranged into seven, nine, or 12 dimensions. Most humans are aware of themselves in the 3rd dimension.

MAKING YOUR OWN MAP

As you begin exploring consciousness, the only thing that matters is your own map. Knowing the rules of maps, if you are using other people's maps, can be useful. But even more useful is remembering that you're never stuck in a map. Everything is equally real and everything is equally illusion. If you are in a map you have a choice: you can work within the parameters of the map you're in, or you can exit the map and replace it with another.

Tips for Making Your Own Map

Many people think of their maps in spatial terms, as would make sense for someone within the 3rd dimension. The 3rd dimension conceptually biases us to arrange things in relation to other things, much as we would arrange a room of furniture. You can arrange your consciousness however you choose. Start from the bottom and go up. Or start at the left and go right. Or arrange things in a 360 degree sphere around you.

Because your map is not likely to look like someone else's, it may be challenging to share your individual map with others. You may spend months just explaining to someone else what your reference and arrangement is. When I first began to explore, I pinned blank sets of newsprint to my wall. I would then position parallel universes or higher dimensions wherever it made sense for me to do so. However, I quickly felt limited with the 2-dimensional paper.

An Alternate Map Technique

Another useful way of creating maps is a template approach. Each map has its own template, or series of templates, depending on the complexity of the map. Thus instead of "going" somewhere in my awareness, I simply bring the awareness to me. I can pull in the Tree of Life Template, for example, and then enter the sphere of Yesod, by accessing that part of the template.

As you begin to create your own map, you may want to ask yourself which maps you resonate with the most and start there. As you explore the map, simply notice where you see differences from the descriptions you've read or heard about. Noticing differences doesn't mean that you're not doing it right! It simply means you're noticing how your individual map works. All the information needed to create your own map of reality is within yourself. Ask your questions when you are in the *now* moment and exploring; the answers will become clear. If the map of your own reality has its limitations, then you are always able to revise and redraw it.

What types of limitations might you run into when using maps? Well many maps are based on assumptions. One assumption might be that the map is positioned within a dualistic space. Thus, you may run into "bad" energies or beings there. If you notice that happening, then you can back out of that map and choose another. Sometimes a map does not allow the option for any possibility other than what is present on the map. This is a common limitation. In my own maps, I always have representations for other possibilities beyond what I am currently aware of, which tends to make my maps very flexible.

Mapping Your Middle World

If you work in the healing field, you will probably need a functional map of the middle world—the world you live in terms of energy. It is in this middle place that it is most useful to have maps that overlap well with other people's maps. This allows your clients to understand to some degree what you are saying to them.

Since maps of anatomy are commonly used, a general understanding of the nervous system, the musculoskeletal system, and so on will serve you well if you are planning to help others as a healing practitioner. Of course, understanding energy fields can also serve, as you can work with these in 3-D and notice useful effects.

There are several very good books that enumerate the following energy field maps: meridians, chakras, layers of the aura, geological fields (leylines, etc), and morphogenetic fields. You would do well to study these so that you have some common language with other practitioners and clients. In addition to *Ascension Magic* by Christopher Penczak, I also recommend *The Subtle Body* by Cyndi Dale.

Question, Explore, Invent, Experiment

Mapping is really where you get to be the discoverer and explorer. What you learn from your experiments may turn out to be very useful to others. Don't sell yourself short by believing that you must follow other people's maps. While their maps may be very useful, helping you move more quickly into unknown realms, realize that they always contain biases that are unique to their creator. Your exploration without these biases may lead you to discover amazing worlds that the original map creator may have missed. Your unique experiences and perspectives can offer a lot to this field of knowledge. Don't think that you're a beginner, with nothing of your own to add. That would be a disservice to everyone. So be inspired to explore!

4

FINDING THE
PLACE OF POWER

THE POINT OF POWER

There is a point, a place, where you gain leverage over old patterns that you want to change. When you stand in this point of power, and make a choice, suddenly old patterns unravel so completely that you wonder how you could have ever been concerned about them in the first place. So where is this point of power and how do you get there? Well, I've noticed this point emerging for me again and again during my evolution.

Let me tell you a specific story to highlight this point of power. It may be surprising to learn that most of my life I suffered from chronic depression. This was a 30-year ongoing reality for me, and the thought of living another 30 years the same way was, quite honestly, a little tiring. For one reason or another, I kept moving along this path of discovering my true self, little by little. What would happen is that I would do something—see a healer, read a book, practice a meditation—and the energy generated would shift things a little, and I would feel a little better. I would then become more optimistic, think more positively, and use the new tool to try to create more of the life I imagined I wanted. For a period of time success and happiness would ensue, but eventually I'd find myself back in the throes of depression again, wondering why I couldn't make "it" last. For the most part, I would hunker down, ride it out until I found another book, healer, or meditation, and the process would continue again. You might notice this type of roller coaster pattern in yourself or in your clients.

This is a useful process! Don't berate yourself if you find yourself on this roller coaster ride with whatever pattern you are trying to change. Each tool you learn, each bit of progress, teaches you something. The first thing I noticed was an ability to be "in" the depression pattern and also simultaneously observe it. I would be able to remember while I was "in it" that the pattern would pass if I let it, and the ride up the coaster would happen again. But one day something different happened. I was presented with the "point of power." The point of power is, quite simply, a place where a choice presents itself.

The point of power happened for me as I was sitting in my room, feeling the depths of depression again. This time the bottom of the roller coaster was a pretty low dip. I heard a voice in my head say, *You've been spending the last several years trying to become enlightened, learning tools that are supposed to help you get a happy life, and look at you now! You are still here in the same place you've always been. You might as well give up!* The despair was rich and I could easily see myself going into it. But then I heard a small, tiny, weak voice. It said, in a pathetically thin and uncertain way, *I don't want this to be true.* What was sad was how powerless that little voice of hope seemed. It was so thin and weak, it sounded like a pathetic wish for the impossible.

There it was, in its saddest form: a choice. I could go into despair, or I could choose to side with this thin, small hope that maybe something could be different. So I chose to turn my awareness in the direction of that pathetic voice which didn't want the old pattern to be true. As unconvincing as that voice sounded, it was my savior. Almost immediately that depression pattern untangled and dropped away—because I chose something different. And that wasn't the only time. Over and over, I've noticed that we struggle with these patterns, doing what we can, and eventually, when we develop the ability to observe ourselves, the point of power emerges and the choice presents itself.

All along we've been told that our experience is a choice. However, until the point of power emerges, we will not be able to see how we keep choosing the painful pattern. Practice the exercises in this text that allow you to observe yourself in the moments when you are at your worst. Then keep alert for the point of power to emerge because at that moment you have the power to define yourself and your life. Although this point can emerge anywhere, the choice made is most powerful in moments of crisis. It is one thing to be happy and joyful and declare you will not experience depression again; but it is quite another thing to be able to make an empowered choice when you are deep in the vortex of depression. These moments are literally the places of great transformation.

IT HAPPENS WHEN YOU LEAST SUSPECT

The crucial moment of choice can happen when you least expect it. Another point of power came for me one night as I returned from a trip, tired from cross-country travel. I arrived to find my beloved cat missing. I spent a sleepless night and began the process of looking throughout the neighborhood early the next day. I happened upon some workers who were making repairs to a house down the street, and asked one of them, "Have you seen a lost cat?" The man replied, "Oh the black and white one? She was in the street and a man stopped in a maroon Cadillac and picked her up and sped off with her." Oh my! This was not news I wanted to hear. My head was full of unhappy thoughts: *It's two days before Halloween, and she's not all black, but could be with a little dye. A lost cat is one thing, but a stolen cat is going to be much harder to find!* My heart was heavy, as this cat had been my companion for seventeen years. I wanted to be with her until the end so I could see her off on her next adventure.

My brain was muddled, jet-lagged, and completely incapable of even writing down the number of the animal shelter. Still, I kept hearing in my thoughts. *This is a test. Why,* I thought, *do I need a test?* Well the truth was that I created miracles easily for clients in my office. However I wasn't used to tapping into miracles for my own personal life. I had certain rules for my clients and different rules for myself. I had no idea what I was going to learn from this experience, but at first I tried to reason my way out of it. *I'm in no shape to try to change my reality right now,* I told myself. I went about in a haze putting up signs around the neighborhood with pictures and the words "Stolen Cat" and a description of the car.

Finally, because I had nothing left to do, and I had not found anyone else who had seen the cat or the car that picked her up, I walked into my meditation room and sat down. I became still and quiet. Then I moved my awareness deep inside, searching for the part of me that had created this rather dramatic situation. I found the pattern, and as soon as I touched it with my awareness, I felt a huge ripping, as if the fabric of space-time itself had been torn. Then stillness. The entire thing had taken just a minute or two. I sat there wondering what else I could do. Surely, there was something else that I should do to help my cat. But my mind was blank. So I reached for the phone to call a friend, but before I could touch it, it rang. On the other end was my next-door neighbor. "Did you find your cat?" he asked. "No, have you seen her?" I replied. "Well, yesterday I saw her in the street. I picked her up and dropped her in front of your house," he said. Then he added, referring to my stolen cat sign, "Oh, and my Cadillac is blue, not maroon." I was stunned. To go from a stolen cat to a lost cat was a wonderful development! I had somehow shifted the universe just enough to create a different result for my cat, and apparently for the color of my neighbor's car too!

Then doubts began to seep into my still-muddled thinking. It probably wasn't something I did. The worker up the street was just mistaken about what happened. Eyewitnesses aren't very reliable, after all. My brain was searching for ways to explain this little miracle away. Then it struck me—this was the point of power! This was my choice, my test, right here. I could opt for a reasonable explanation, or I could accept that I was amazingly powerful in my world. This was a crucial choice that ended up altering my life immensely. I'm sure you can guess the choice I made that day. I chose to step fully into my power and own that I am responsible for my reality. It was the most important choice I have ever made!

My cat was back in my arms two hours later. As I walked down the street calling for my now lost cat, I saw a sign: "Found, black and white cat." She lived another three years and then passed away gracefully with me by her side, just as I had wanted. But my life was irrevocably changed. No longer did I see my personal life as separate from my professional life. No longer did I see my personal self as limited in any way. This was the true beginning of living in limitlessness, with just one seamless existence full of grace and magic.

FEAROLOGY

One of the biggest limitations we all face, as we try to find this point of power, is fear. No one escapes this limitation in some form or another. Once, early in my consciousness studies, I was ruminating on the idea of power. I decided I would look for my power in a meditation. Once still and quiet, I looked around and saw a ladder leading up. I climbed for a very long time up beyond the clouds, and came to the edge of a wall. Over that wall, I knew I would find my power. I peered over that wall, and what I saw struck instant fear in my heart. My power, it seemed, went on for as far as the eye could see into infinity. I quickly climbed down that ladder, a bit awestruck. Awesome power does require an awesome responsibility. Was I ready for that?

Meta-rule sets can help to control thoughts in our head that stop us from exploring our power. It is true that some of these thoughts are based on deeper issues that relate to fears—not being good enough is a common example. But when the issue really strikes a deeper chord with us than just a thought or belief that is holding us back, then we may have to resort to other tools. Sometimes a simple meta-rule that states "It does not matter whether I'm afraid or not, it will not affect the outcome" may be all the courage we need to move into the activity that is causing fearful emotions. But if not, have no fear (ha!) as I have other tools.

Indeed fear is something that I have studied very closely for some time; you could possibly refer to me as a "fearologist." Fear has attracted my close attention ever since an incident that occurred many years ago. A mentor told me that if I wanted to know what my destiny in this world was, all I needed to do was to sit in meditation and in that space, walk down a road, and meet my future self coming in the other direction. I could ask this future self what my destiny was, and I would get an answer. So I did this meditation and when I met my future self, I was told the following: "Your purpose is to lead people through their fear. Fear is the root of all the problems on your planet. Indeed the opposite of love is not hate, but fear. Hate is simply one form of fear. In fact, the reason we do not experience peace on Earth is solely because of fear."

When I first heard these words I really didn't know how I would ever apply the concept of "leading people through their fear" in my life. But I walked away from that meditation with a firm knowledge that fear is simply an illusion. And because I "knew" that fear was not real, I was less affected by it in everyday situations. What do I mean by that? I mean that I understood that being afraid wasn't a valid excuse. This was the single most important idea that helped me move beyond fear.

Fear Is Not an Identity

Why would we ever come to believe that fear is a valid excuse? Often we become so accustomed to our fears that we allow them to create identities for us. Let's say I'm afraid of speaking in front of groups. I might tell myself, *Well I don't like being in front of large groups; it's just not my personality; I'm not an attention-getter; I prefer smaller more intimate settings which feel more real to me.* Thus, I construct a whole identity around a fear which helps to maintain the fear. I can believe that this is simply the way I am. But if I were to look more closely, I would see that I have boxed myself in and shut myself off from experiences and opportunities that might be good for me. If this sounds like you, then becoming free of fear doesn't mean that your personality will shift radically and you'll become a rock star speaker. But you will feel that you have the choice, that you can easily and comfortably experience being in front of a group. Even though you may still prefer small, intimate groups, you will not be limited to them.

When we are not limited by our fears, we can make discerning choices, weighing out the pros and cons of a situation. An example of this was a hapkido class I took after my back surgery. I had back surgery because of a debilitating martial arts injury that had not healed after about two years of near constant pain. The surgery itself was successful, but I was left with a great deal of fear because that injury was so debilitating—not just physically, but mentally and emotionally as well. I was very afraid of reinjury. To make matters worse, I had a number of doctors making lists of things I could *never* do again because now I would be even more susceptible to reinjury of a similar kind! I didn't want to create an identity out of my back injury. So about one year post-surgery, I signed up for a hapkido class, which involves a lot of falling, throwing, and rolling! If you're afraid of falling, what better activity to choose than one that requires you to fall?

One afternoon the instructor decided we would learn how to fall from a throw. He would send us into a flip, feet over our head, and we would land on the floor. Needless to say, I was a bit skeptical about whether this was a good idea. Maybe I should sit this one out! But my instructor thought it would be safe, despite my previous injuries. And so I made a decision, that if I was going to do this activity, I would do it 100%. I knew that any hesitation—any holding back on my part or fear of hurting myself—would make the scenario of hurting myself much more likely. And so I stepped up to the mat and went flying through the air, landing safely and with pretty darn near perfect form! The instructor blinked and said, "Wow! That's just about the best first landing I've ever seen!" Whew! Well I don't make it a point to go flying through the air on a regular basis, but I am glad I was able to do it once.

Fear of pain is a biological mechanism designed to keep our physical bodies safe, and yet we can overcome it if we like. Other fears include the fear of death, which is often comprised of a mix of biological and psychological components, and the fear of an event such as speaking in front of a group, meeting new people, or being vulnerable in a relationship. Now, we can analyze why we fear something, and delve into self-esteem issues and such, but working through these deeper issues takes time. I will be showing you a shortcut.

My philosophy has always been to take the easiest path through fears, to not give them a lot of energy as I easily shift them and free myself from their snares. If you find that you want to hold on to a fear, and cling to the identity that you've built around it, then you will need to recognize that this part of you that wants to cling is just your ego. It is not who you are, but rather an identity that you are not neutral to, as we discussed earlier. If you find this is the case for you, you can use the "Dispersing the Emotional Vortex" exercise from Chapter 2 to create a neutral state that will allow you to more fully let go of the fear.

Future Fear

Finally, let's consider "worry" which is a very common type of fear that is centered around the future. When we worry, we project lack or pain or whatever the issue is into the future. This projection prevents us from enjoying the moment right now. Indeed, if you examine this moment right now as you are reading this, you might realize that you are breathing, most likely sitting somewhere warm and comfortable, and have eaten in the last twelve hours or so. In fact you have everything you need right now. Worrying about tomorrow will simply cause you to miss how perfect right now is. Even if you're reading on an airplane and a baby is crying nearby, even if you're on a bus and it's a wet day and you're feeling slightly damp, these slight annoyances are all a part of a relatively comfortable now. Of course if you are reading this from a war zone, by all means, put this book down, and run for cover! However, if you tend to worry about future events, even though your now is quite comfortable, then you may want to use these fears in the exercises that follow.

I won't go into all the other types of fears, as the ones I've mentioned here are very common, and should give you enough ideas to play with. However, just because I didn't mention a specific fear that you have, doesn't mean you can't play with it in the following exercises. Remember, you want to experiment and modify the exercises to suit your needs, as any intrepid explorer of consciousness would!

MOVING BEYOND FEAR

As you move forward into this section, remember this: much more can be gained by moving through your fears than you ever imagined. As you move towards your full power, along the way you will find great gifts in the spaces that you have not yet dared to tread, just waiting there for you. I find these edges of my own self so productive in my expansion pursuits—that when I feel fear these days, I know it is showing me the best direction to grow and expand myself. Fears are the places where I am limited; they demarcate the edges of my box. By moving beyond them, I grow exponentially, and have access to entire worlds I could have never imagined—worlds that were blocked by the darkness of my fear. Now when I feel fear, I think, *Wow, I'm scared of that! How interesting!* And I get curious, as curiosity is an excellent perspective from which to explore fear.

Now that you have perhaps identified a fear or two, I want to share a few different methods to work with them. Remember our goal is to shift a fear pattern enough so that we gain freedom and choice, and are no longer limited by the fear. In the beginning, and especially for fears such as the fear of events (speaking, meeting new people, etc.), you may need to do what I did, which is to just do the fearful thing anyway. However, I'll offer a few tips to allow you to shortcut some of the steps I had to take. Most people probably think that the best option when faced with a fear is to change the fear, and then do the activity that was previously fearful. However, often the quickest way to your goal is directly through the "problem." There are two important things to remember if you decide to take this route: 1) that fear is an illusion and 2) that fear is not a valid excuse.

The Illusion of Fear

First, get it very clear in your mind that fear is an illusion. As you go through the fear you will eventually accumulate enough evidence that this is the case, and your fear will stand down. I learned this important lesson through my martial arts training, which was quite rigorous and involved full contact sparring classes. The prospect of being hit can provoke fear in most people. In addition to that fear, I found I was also afraid of hitting or hurting someone else. As I participated in these classes over and over, eventually I was faced with overwhelming evidence that neither hitting nor being hit was as terrible as I thought. The panic then subsided, and suddenly, overnight I became a much better fighter because I was no longer afraid. One of my opponents noticed, remarking "What happened? You're kicking my ass!" To which I replied, "I'm simply no longer afraid of you!" Indeed, each rank test, in addition to a demonstration of skill and technique, was designed to push me into that edge of fear. Eventually, when I realized I would not die from any test nor would anyone else, the gig was up. The test then became pointless.

Second, if you find yourself hesitating at the idea of moving directly into your fears, you will want to use the mantra: Fear is not a valid excuse. Often, as I work with students wanting to create healing practices, I will suggest that they do live demos and speak in front of people, discussing and demonstrating whatever type of healing work they do. The most common response to that idea is "Oh, I'm afraid to speak in front of groups." My first thought, is always, *so?* For years we have accepted these limitations and they have become our identity. Even if we are comfortable and not feeling much fear, we will say we can't do something because we are afraid. When we stop and listen more closely, and decide that fear is not a valid excuse, we have to move differently. A path that has not been open to us before has just now come into view, and now it is just a matter of navigating through it. We can remind ourselves that fear is just an illusion, and therefore it isn't a valid excuse, and we can move into the activity anyway, in spite of our fears. Why would we accept a limitation that keeps us from being successful in our chosen work that we are so passionate about? Nike was on to something when they claimed the tag line, Just Do It.

Why not just move the fear pattern first? Well, I have seen many people attempt to do this, yet find themselves mired for years in endless layers of the pattern. It is almost as if the ego makes the game as complicated as possible to keep them from having to face the thing they believe they are afraid of! While I will show you some tools to move the patterns themselves, I recommend working on both levels—using the tools to shift the fears and doing the activity that provokes the fear regardless. By working on many levels at once, you will more quickly bust these fear patterns!

Once you have considered doing the activity that scares you, you may use the following tools to explore and shift the fear patterns prior to doing the activity itself. There are a couple of useful meditative exercises. One is specific and one is non-specific. Both have their benefits, and so I will discuss both here.

EXERCISE

Fear-Busting Rehearsal

When something frightens us, our body is conditioned to respond with a cascade of responses. We refer to this set of responses as "fight or flight." When visualizing, the physical body does not know the difference between a real or imaginary situation, so it responds as if the situation is real. We can use this tendency to shift our reaction to something that usually causes fear. This is a way for us to face our fear prior to the actual event.

- Imagine the event that causes the fear in as much detail as possible.

- Notice where the emotion of fear arises. Often people notice it in their throat, their gut, their heart, but it can be anywhere.

- Bring the emotion to neutral. How do you bring an emotion to neutral? Choose from many ways:
  - Push your awareness though the discomfort;
  - Untangle the feeling until it subsides;
  - Notice the direction the feeling moves, and run its movement in the opposite direction; or
  - Focus on your breathing until it subsides.
- Play with the above until you find what works for you.
- Bring your attention back to imagining the event, and repeat.
- Notice how the fear is different the next time you imagine it. Continue until you have no fearful emotion when imagining it!
- Maybe this takes you only one time, or ten times, or 100 times. Continue to notice how it is different each time. It has been my experience that as you get used to shifting things in this way, fewer repetitions will be needed.

EXERCISE

Seeing through the Illusion of Fear

This meditation illustrates the point that fear is just an illusion blocking you from freedom. In some ways this meditation is simpler because it doesn't require neutralizing the emotion that comes up. I've been using variations on this meditation for years, for everything from changing a fearful situation to getting inspirational ideas to accessing possible futures. Again, your impetus to play around with these tools will mean that you can get a lot out of them. Here's one basic way to do this meditation when dealing with a fear you have:

- Get relaxed and imagine yourself lying under a beautiful tree near a meadow. Allow the sounds and sensations of the scene to become vivid and real.

- Once you are comfortable under the tree, allow your "physical" body to rest protected there, as you get up and move about the meadow. Notice the details of your meadow.

- Eventually you will find a path leading through the woods. Follow this path.

- As you follow the path, notice the sensory details— sounds and smells—of the woods. You will eventually come to a clearing.

- In the clearing is a very large crystal, the size of a small building, jutting up out of the earth. Walk up to the crystal and appreciate its beauty and structure.

- Place one hand along one of the walls of the crystal. Notice how you can feel the vibration of the crystal. Allow your hand to match this vibration.

- As your hand matches the vibration, your entire body follows and also matches the vibration. Once this happens, you notice how easy it is to simply walk through the wall into the interior of the crystal.

• Once inside, explore to your heart's content! There are many rooms, and the spaces here do not follow the rules of the 3-D world outside.

• Eventually, you will come to a room with a beautiful pool of water. Rest along the mossy banks. In this quiet space, you can feel the safety and comfort of nature as it is here to help you and teach you.

• In this room is also a door. Behind the door resides your fear. When you eventually go through the door you will be able to learn about this fear, and possibly receive messages or information that you need to help release it. Know that as you explore your fear from this space, nothing can hurt you.

• When you are ready, enter the room. Notice how the fear appears. Is the room dark or murky? Is the air thick or thin? Notice the details of whatever is in the room, knowing that it is contained in these walls and you are completely safe. Ask questions as if you are interviewing the fear. See what information it has for you.

• Eventually, make your way across the room and find a door on the other side. When you open this door, you will discover what lies beyond your fear.

• Go ahead and open the door, and move into the room that lies beyond your fear. Notice the details. Is the room bright or colorful? Is the air sweet or thick? What feeling do you get when you are in this space? How do feel now that you have walked through your fear and have reached the other side?

• As you move about in the space beyond your fear, you will eventually notice another door. It is not the same door that you used to enter. When you are ready, you can open that door and find yourself back on the mossy banks of the beautiful pool of water.

• Once on the mossy bank, meditate for a while on what you have learned here.

• When you are ready, leave the crystal the same way you entered. When you find the entrance, place your hand on the wall of the crystal and allow your hand, and then your body to match the vibration.

• Once outside the crystal, follow the path back through the woods to the meadow, and eventually to the tree.

• Connect once more to your "physical" body that is sleeping comfortably under the tree. Feel the ground again, as you find yourself lying under the tree.

• When you are ready, open your eyes, and say out loud "Awake."

Feel free to change the above meditation, making it longer or shorter as you need. Ideally, you should not rush through the experience. Give yourself ample time for things that you are not aware of to drift into the experience. The slower you go, the more you will learn in the meditation.

❖ ❖ ❖

The final tool I will share is the simplest one of all, though it may be a stretch for you if you have not yet gathered momentum of consciousness through working on all the previous exercises. Once you have some experience, you can make these processes happen much more quickly. However, skipping the early exercises means you will not have integrated the skills to a point where they are automatic.

In my earlier career, I spent much time teaching English to students from other countries. I used to give them what seemed like very tedious exercises to go through each paragraph— sentence by sentence, and word by word, asking and thinking about whether that phrase or sentence followed the rules we were learning. If they did this once or twice, they would quickly find that they noticed whether something was right or wrong in the process of writing it, and they could make adjustments then. Finally they would be able to skip the tedious slow part, natu- rally writing things correctly because they had taken the time to slowly work each skill. You too will notice that you can't really skip the first stages in consciousness expansion just because they require a little focus and effort. However, once you do take that time and get the foundation, then your consciousness begins to respond automatically. You don't have to think it through, and you don't have to even work hard at it. Shifting and changing your patterns will simply become a natural thing that you do!

It's the same with these exercises as well; though many peo- ple believe that if you don't work hard, you can't let go of a fear pattern or move beyond it. Not true! Once you have the basic foundation, you can do many things just naturally. However, you will have to let go of that old human habit of believing that everything takes work. You may need to trust that the time you spent building your foundation was really all that was necessary. Then you can simply substitute the idea that something is true because you say it is! And then test it! Don't believe something if all your experiences contradict it, but notice how many experiences don't contradict it. If you find that what you say will happen, doesn't always, then get curious, explore, and figure out why that may be so for you!

Based on this principle that things are super simple once you've mastered the foundation, I will now share the simplest way of all to change a fear pattern. I hate to even call it a meditation, because I don't see it that way. But here it goes: As soon as you become aware of a fear pattern, think: *Oh, that's interesting . . . Let's see how that changes now.* Then forget about it! A week or two later, check in. Think about that fear and notice how it has changed. Often I only need to do this once, but I've had lots of practice. If it hasn't changed enough to my satisfaction, then I will simply do it again. It's so simple, why not? If it seems different at all, then you've had a success, so just do it again!

PART TWO

Playing with Consciousness

CHANGING YOURSELF
AND YOUR WORLD

5

EXPANDING
YOUR
PERSONAL POWER

When we embark upon the path to expand our power in the world of consciousness, we need to understand that this path is more of an *undoing* than a *doing*. Most accomplishments that we achieve in the world are outward expressions of our self. But in the world of consciousness, the places of power are largely internal. Our conscious awareness expands when we let go and surrender our small, ego-self. This ego-self which was so useful in expanding our outer world can be a hindrance when expanding our consciousness. I remember struggling with ego at one point, wanting very much to extract, kill, and bury it! But without the small ego, we would have little motivation for creating in this world. Instead of destroying it, we need to allow it to move into balance with our authentic self. This way we can choose to move into ego as we interact and create, and out of ego when we need access to our consciousness beyond the typical 3-D experience.

HEARING YOUR GUIDANCE

In the first part of this book, we practiced moving our awareness and expanding our consciousness. Now it's time to apply these abilities to change our life. As we begin our search to expand our consciousness, one of the first things we notice is that others seem to have access to information beyond the ordinary. Since this is often attributed to guides, we also desire to hear, see, or understand our guides. Indeed, one of the questions I am most often asked is "How did you learn to hear your guides?" The short answer is really this: I practiced tools like the ones I presented to you in the first part of the book, getting out of my head and into my heart. The guidance we are looking for is far easier to notice in this heart-space of awareness. Indeed, it has always been there, just waiting for us to tune in.

I want to discuss in depth the need to have a sense of guidance we can count on, since this is an important milestone as we expand our consciousness. Many people who claim to not hear their guides—including me in the beginning—have difficulty only because their expectations get in the way. One reason our expectations around this concept are so screwed up is because of the limitations of our language. Language is not and cannot be accurate in conveying the concepts that I am about to discuss here. No matter how I try to explain it, a reader is likely to go away with some misconceptions. This is one area that you are going to have to discover inside yourself; I can only point in the general direction.

One area where language can be problematic is when we attempt to define the concept of guides. If I tell you that I can hear my guides, what does that mean? People often believe that guides are beings or entities that exist separate and distinct from themselves. Perhaps they are more "knowing" beings who are somehow more aware and conscious than we are here on Earth. People believe that these higher beings are instructing them by passing information to them. Some people go so far as to say that there are several levels of guides, and as you progress in your own evolution and awareness you "graduate" to new guides—sort of like being passed up the ladder of ascension. Other people believe they are in contact with other notable beings such as angels or ascended masters. And some people simply define their guide as being their higher self.

I, for one, do not really care who gets credit for this guidance; I simply wish to have access to the information I need. I don't quibble over these definitions, but for me guidance most often feels like my access to my greater Self. Occasionally information seems to come from another conscious entity or entities, but for me that is rare. Most information that I access daily seems to be from just a greater aspect of me—or perhaps of all of us. It quickly becomes clear as you explore these worlds of consciousness that this information is not available only to one person. Indeed, we all seem to be connected to this larger field.

Some people report experiencing their guides as fully present, appearing as images in front of them and talking to them. If you have experienced guides this way, then count yourself lucky because this, as far as I can tell, is highly unusual! This may be my own bias, however, since I rarely experience guides this way.

In fact, the couple of experiences I have had with beings appearing directly in front of me, startled me so thoroughly that I now have a rule that such beings can only appear as hazy forms, and never as solid beings.

The first time I saw a guide in solid form was long before I had any foundation in consciousness studies or explorations. I was simply trying to meditate, and had no idea how. During one of my attempts, I was sitting alone in my bedroom. As I meditated by staring at a flickering candle in the dark, my vision completely faded. When it returned several beings were sitting there with me! Well, I was shocked, as I thought I was completely alone, and I quickly jolted myself out of the meditation. To avoid the feeling of being mentally ill, I changed the rules so that such an appearance wouldn't happen again. Many of us are not ready for our reality to abruptly change.

As a result of my rule, I do not experience seeing guides in solid form at all. Yet many people, I believe, have the expectation that this is the way it must occur for them to have access to their guides. Such expectations can really mess you up, causing you to miss the way your guides are already helping you. Just because you never experience guides as solid beings, doesn't mean that you don't have access to the information they provide. I, for one, was unaware of the ways I was already connected to my guides for quite some time before I realized that something was happening in that arena. The story of how I became aware is really quite funny.

I became aware of my guides during my martial arts training. My instructor at the time used to coach us with the words, "listen, listen, listen." Listening in the martial arts is not about

hearing with your ears, but being aware of your opponent energetically with a very expanded awareness. This was also one way
the instructor would move us into the no-mind space. Listening
was all about being completely open, and not thinking. If you
were hearing the thoughts in your head, then you were not listening. Once out of your head, listening became much easier.
Suddenly it became apparent where the opponent was going to
move before they moved. Most of the listening occurred with
your awareness centered in their chest, and a simultaneous "feeling" sense with whatever part of the body was in contact with
the opponent, often the forearms. If you "listened" with your
forearms, for example, you gained all kinds of awareness you
would have otherwise overlooked. In short, good listening in the
martial arts is all about expanding your awareness.

I was highly motivated to practice listening to become a better fighter. But imagine my surprise as I began to see this skill
showing up in the rest of my life as well. I noticed that as I listened to people talk, if I was listening from the awareness of
my heart, I would hear what a person said, overlaid with what
they meant to say or wanted to say, but didn't. This confused me
because I heard two things. Which was the one they said, and
which did they merely think? I had to stop and think before I
responded. I needed to make sure I was responding to the correct thing! Because the overlapping information was giving me
trouble, I wondered if maybe there was an easier way to "hear."
At that point, I began to hear a specific ring when someone said
something that was true. That ring was absent if something
wasn't true. Later on I was able to make finer distinctions. For
example, when something being said was not true, I could tell

whether the speaker thought she was telling the truth or knew she was not.

In addition, hunches and intuitions, always accompanied by a specific feeling in my body, became reliable ways to judge what to do or not do. Of course, I made some errors along the way. Ignoring an intuitive feeling that I should not take my car on a trip to California was one such time. Despite the fact that I took the car to the mechanic to prep it for the trip, the car almost caught on fire going over the mountains in Southern Oregon, and I had to have it towed. Well, lesson learned! Almost. I had at least one more incident where I didn't listen to that feeling, and things didn't turn out so well. So I made a pact with myself: trust that feeling no matter what! And I still do to this day.

But are feelings, intuition, and hunches the same thing as hearing your guides? I think these are definitely some of the ways that our guidance speaks to us. My father, for example, doesn't pay much attention to any of these new age ideas. But even he has admitted to believing in angels since, on more than one occasion, something clued him in with a strong enough feeling that he was able to avoid a catastrophe. If you've had these types of experiences, then you should know you are already hearing your guides!

The term "hearing" is inadequate and entirely incorrect when you consider that the sense of hearing itself refers to the receptors in the ear transferring an impulse to the brain that can be interpreted. Indeed, your guides will not likely be able to stimulate those actual receptors. Your brain may still interpret information in words in a manner that replicates hearing, or perceiving thoughts in your head. This explains why originally, this kind of information gathering was referred to as "ESP" or extra-sensory perception: you don't actually use your physical sense organs.

In my case, I finally became aware of hearing information from somewhere else because my guides had a conversation with me about pig orgasms! This very unusual conversation happened one day while I was doing some bookkeeping, alone, at the martial arts school. I remembered having a conversation about pig orgasms, and I thought to myself: *Well that's very odd. What an unusual topic. And really, who could I have had that conversation with?* The question plagued me for a bit, and then I decided to see if I had just imagined this story about pigs having 30-minute orgasms. I did a quick internet search, and sure enough I found websites, however unscientific, that made this claim! So I was curious. How could I, out of the blue, with no one else physically in the room, become aware of such an odd statistic as that? My guides, it would seem, had been giving me information all along. But they had to get a little bit crazy for me to finally notice and become aware! Guides, it seems, have a pretty good sense of humor!

You may already be hearing your guides, and discounting the information because it doesn't seem to be your idea of what a guide would say. I was working with an apprentice at one of my workshops, when she told me that she wanted to hear her guides. So during the session, I literally tuned her vibration to the space where she could hear her guides. When I asked her what she noticed, she responded, "Nothing, I still don't hear anything!" Well, this was totally embarrassing for me, to say the least! But, sometimes that happens in sessions. Sometimes your client won't notice any changes. But, at the next day of the workshop, I asked her to provide more feedback to the participants. How was she feeling about the session, now that some time had passed? To which she sheepishly replied, "Well, on the way over here, I heard a voice say, 'Kiss the angel!' And I was kind of confused. But then I realized I had a little angel figurine in my car, so I grabbed it and kissed it, and I suddenly became aware that I *did* hear things yesterday, after we had the session. But they weren't the profound things I imagined guides and higher being would pontificate on, so I assumed that wasn't it!"

What are the specific signs, then, that guides are communicating with you? I believe each person will have unique experiences in this matter, so again, you will want to look inside for your answers. But in my own development I've noticed the following: hearing information overlaid on top of what is being said; hearing a ring sound that indicates what is true in that moment (note: some people experience goose bumps when they hear something true); and a thought that moves through my head that seems to come from elsewhere and that has an accompanying feeling. What feeling am I speaking of? Well, words are highly inadequate here, so you should not attach too much weight to how I describe it, but instead allow your own experience to emerge. That said, I feel flush or full, as if there is an alignment or flow that accompanies that thought. Also, I may notice a series of synchronicities around an idea. For example, three different and unrelated people may mention a word or idea within a short span of a week or so. This is usually an indication for me to pay attention to this idea. However, since your experience will be unique to you, try the following exercise to practice your "listening" skills.

The "Choosing from Your Heart" exercise was one of the very early tools that I used to help me develop my listening skills. Listening cannot happen from the head. If you are quite logical, you may be used to thinking through the pros and cons of an action and then making a choice. I also use my head in many situations and make choices based on logical pros and cons. But often the pros and cons aren't clearly stacked, and I may feel that the logical mind can't make a clear choice. This is the ideal time to use this technique. In addition, I check my heart even when the choice seems obvious from a logical, left-brained perspective.

More than anything, this is one tool that helped me learn to listen and be aware of things outside of my head. You can start with something easy, like a lunch menu. That way, there are no real consequences to making an "incorrect" choice, outside of getting an item that you might not like.

EXERCISE

Choosing from Your Heart

Have a list of your choices at hand. You may write the choices on separate pieces of paper, if that works better for you.

- First spend some time getting into a meditative, quiet, grounded state. Notice your heart field. Think of your favorite person, pet, or thing and allow that thought to expand your heart field until you feel good.

- Next, place one of the choices in your hand. This can be written on a piece of paper or you can simply "put" the thought of the choice in your hand.

- Bring the hand up to your heart field.

- Notice what happens. Does the heart field change? Does it get warmer or cooler? Does it expand or constrict? Does it stay exactly the same?

- Try this with each of your choices and notice what happens. I usually look for a warmer or more expanded heart field. However your personal cues may be different, so don't rely on how it works for me. Notice carefully how it works for you.

- Lastly, hold a final choice named "something else" up to your heart field. Sometimes none of the choices are the right one. You may need to wait for "something else" to show up.

One example of how the "Choosing from Your Heart" exercise worked really well for me was when I was looking for office space for my practice. I looked at quite a few spaces and found two potential spaces. I wrote down all the pros and cons of each, but I really wasn't getting a clear indication from my head of which would be the best choice. So I did the above exercise, and held both choices before my heart. However, neither one had much of an effect on my heart field. Sometimes this means that it doesn't matter. The choice of office will not actually have any effect in my world positively or negatively. But that wasn't the case here. When I held the "something else" choice in front of my heart field, I got a huge expansion! It wasn't easy turning down both spaces, because at the time I didn't have a third option. But I trusted my heart and let both offices go. A few weeks later, I happened upon an office space for lease that had everything I wanted in my next office space! In addition, this office was exceedingly inexpensive! Fabulous! I was right to wait for something else, and can thank this exercise for making that clear to me.

One caution about this exercise, however, is to pay attention to fear responses. If a choice brings up a fear reaction then you are no longer in your heart-space; you are instantly ungrounded, and you cannot rely on the information. Many people ask, "How do I know that's the right answer, and not just my wishful thinking?" Well, you know by practicing and calibrating your results. Notice whether your choices are pleasing to you or not. You eventually become more confident after noticing which kind of feeling produces which kind of outcome. Practice and calibrate your results here. Your feelings and sensations will not be the same as your neighbor's.

TIPS FOR HEARING YOUR GUIDES

All of the exercises presented so far will connect you to the space where you start noticing the information or guidance that has been there all along. Once you access your heart space, you can cultivate a dialogue with your guides. Use the "Strengthening Your Connection to Guidance" exercise as a starting point. Then, assume that they are around and converse with them, asking them for guidance on the issues you are wondering about. Ask—and allow the answers to emerge, however they emerge. Allow the information to show up in whatever form it does, and release any expectations of it showing up in any certain way.

EXERCISE

Strengthening Your Connection to Guidance

- ◆ Once you are relaxed and centered in a meditative state, imagine a picture of your higher self.

- ◆ Don't censor the image. Whatever comes to mind first is fine. It might look angelic or Buddha-like. It might look like you but larger, or more transparent, or more colorful. It might even look like an inanimate object. Whatever the image, this represents your higher self or guide.

- ◆ Imagine a beam of light connecting you to your higher self.

- ◆ Watch as the light beam grows stronger, brighter, bigger.

- ◆ Do this meditation daily and notice how your daily connection strengthens.

- ◆ Once connected, you can ask questions or ask for guidance.

Since being in the *now* allows you the best access to the information, practicing the exercises in this book that allow you to drop the past and future will be useful. The best, most inspired, and most useful information always comes from being in the flow. When you are open to Source and listening, divine inspiration can easily move through you. If you cultivate this state in your everyday life, and not just in meditation, eventually there will be no distinction between your guides and you. You will *be* the flow of divine inspiration.

Spending more time in higher vibrational states is another way to cultivate an expanded awareness. Much music and art, as well as many energetic gatherings, contain these vibrations that will expand your awareness. As you participate in dance, chanting, toning, energy workshops, and intentional festivals, you will begin to lock into these vibrations and be in them during your everyday life. Living more fully in these expanded states is one way to be in the flow of information as much as possible.

WHAT HAPPENS ONCE YOU HEAR YOUR GUIDES?

Some people believe that they will instantly have a better life because they can hear their guides. They believe that their guides will end uncertainty and eliminate mistakes. They also believe that their guides will always tell them to do things that will make their life easier, better, or richer in some way. Some people want their guides to hand over the lottery numbers! However, you may be surprised to learn that your guides may not be concerned with the same issues that you are.

If you are looking for guidance on a career path, for example, and your guides haven't given you any direction, is it because you can't hear your guides? Maybe not. It could be because, in the larger scheme of things, your career path is irrelevant. However, it has been my experience that hearing my guidance and knowing what I "should" do, does not always make my life easier, simpler, or more flowing. My guides tend to lead me in directions that I'd rather not go—directions that expand me in some way or other, often beyond my own comfort zone.

For example, I have often come across a scenario where I know what I should do, but I don't know how to do it. Well, wouldn't it be nice if guides provided a detailed manual with everything, but they don't seem to in my case! One very specific example is when my guides told me to hold group healing sessions. And eventually I did develop my group Holographic Healing teleconference sessions. But when I first started, I had no idea *how* this was going to work. To be honest, if you're pushing the edges of your own consciousness, there aren't going to be many manuals. Even if someone else has done something similar to what you'd like to do, their way of doing it may not work for you. So trying to replicate what someone else is doing, is not something I would recommend. In truth, no one knows how to do something, until they do it!

Imagine our ancient ancestors, trying to figure out how to cook. Well maybe leaving the meat in the sun wasn't a good idea. Don't do it like that. Maybe you should try this fire thing. Oh that worked well! Now we know how. Someone has to be the experimenter, someone has to give it a try, and that might as well be you! There really is no such thing as failure; if it doesn't work, that's just information that you need to try something else. Don't let it stop you if your guides have pointed you in a direction without specific instructions on how to make it happen. If it is truly your calling, you will figure it out. For my Holographic Healing sessions, I started with a plan that I pieced together from the few things I'd seen others do. But that wasn't what actually happened once I started, so I remained open to how it was unfolding in the moment. In this way I was guided through how to do it, once the session began. Of course this means that you have to really trust that you'll be able to make it up on the spot. This is one way that you can use the ability to let go of your expectations. What emerges organically in the moment, is always the best outcome. Even if you start with a plan, be flexible enough to allow it to morph in front of you.

Another issue that came up for me as I began hearing my guides was this: I would know what I was supposed to do, but for whatever reason, I would be afraid of doing it. I'm talking loosely about fear here. This usually means that I'm afraid of what other people will think if I follow my guides. Consider the story of Noah, for example. Well, perhaps even better is the modern day retelling of the Noah story in the movie *Evan Almighty*. Evan didn't really want to build an ark, even when he was expressly told what to do, because he would be ridiculed by family, co-workers, and the media at large. But he had no other choice.

Generally, I find this to be true: If I go ahead and follow the path I am being led to, things flow smoothly. When I resist it, things can get uncomfortable. And yet, it is often uncomfortable to be in the position where others find you ludicrous. This is how I felt when my guides asked me to offer the Phoenix Consciousness Downloads on my website. I resisted this for a long time because I thought others would question my integrity, or see me as a snake-oil salesman. Yet, when I finally did this, about nine months or so after being told to, I received really positive responses to this new technology that does not have a 3-D object place holder. The goal is to expand people's awareness of what is possible, and I think the program has achieved that. I was unsure how well such a delivery method would work for the goal of actually producing change, but over and over again, people write to me with stories of amazing things that have happened after they interacted with the technology.

Just like an individual session, however, results vary. I had to laugh when one client angrily demanded his money back, claiming that he thought he was getting an mp3 recording, but all he got was my stupid intent! Here it was—the reaction I was most afraid of! But so many people had been quite happy with my stupid intent, that my earlier fears seemed silly now. One person didn't want to try it. And, that is perfect. Each of us will find the right path when we are ready.

Sometimes, luckily, my experience hearing my guides is exactly what most people imagine it would be like to hear their guides. Occasionally, I have an idea presented together with the feeling and knowing that this is the direction I should go in, *and* it also happens to be something I want to do. It's not super common for me to have this type of experience and in fact, if it happened a lot, I would get suspicious. If your guides are always telling you to buy things that you want or to do things that you want to do, you might want to take a closer look at what you are calling your guides. I have heard people criticize others who use the excuse "my guides told me to" as a way of not taking responsibility for their own actions. I do believe that you should examine this aspect of your guidance if you find you jump to the answer "my guides told me to" whenever someone questions your actions or motives. Sometimes, following your guides may make you unpopular, but cultivating discernment about what is an impulse and what is really guided action may be necessary.

In addition, your guides may lead you into situations designed to clean up your issues—what I call being guided to an ego-challenge. This can be a trying situation, because it can cause people to stop listening to their guidance in order to preserve the ego. So what does this type of situation look like? Well, you sense you are being guided to do something, you do it, and it turns out badly—or at least your ego thinks so! If this happens to you, should you fire your guides? Before you do that, look closely at the situation. One of the most important aspects of expanding our awareness involves dropping much of our ego façade.

For example, one client came to me distraught over a breakup. She felt she couldn't trust her guides because she listened to their guidance and opened her heart to this person, who now was abandoning her! However, if she had looked more closely, she may have seen that this is one area where she needed to clean up an issue or two. Being open-hearted for the joy of it, without being attached to a certain response from her lover, may actually have been the lesson her guides were moving her towards.

It is often only after the fact that we realize something we thought we didn't want to happen actually opened the way for amazing new things to enter our lives. But we are quick to condemn ourselves, and lose trust in our connection with Source. In general, our ego gets all bent out of shape. *How could my guides make me do something that is hurtful to me?* Well it might be hurtful to our small egos, but expansive to our overall consciousness, if we are willing to use the information rather than judge that pain-free equals good and challenging equals bad.

Following your guidance in no way guarantees you a pain-free life! Sometimes, in fact, the quickest way to where you want to go involves moving directly through the difficult situations for the learning that will entail. It won't kill you, but your ego might be taken down a notch or two. This will not hurt your self-esteem either. In fact, when the ego drops away, self-esteem is less of an issue, because you are getting closer and closer to an authentic you, which is always 100% awesome.

SHOULD YOU FIRE YOUR GUIDES?

Many people ask me how they can know if their guides can be trusted. This reminds me of a story one of my mentors used to tell about how he would ask his guide which road he should take to get somewhere. He'd listen for the answer, and if he ran into a lot of traffic, then he knew to fire that guide. Well, what I believe he was really doing here was calibrating. He was trying to discern for himself what a correct answer would feel like. There is some practice involved in learning how you personally determine whether something is coming from a higher source than your mind for sure, because everyone is going to have unique sensations and feelings. However, once you are able to determine what a correct response feels like, you will always be able to trust that feeling.

The larger question here is whether you trust yourself, which can also take some practice. I had quite a few car issues, as I mentioned earlier, even though I could have avoided them if I had followed my guidance! Since I started trusting myself and that certain feeling though, I have been able to easily avoid several dicey situations. Just recently, in fact, I was able to avoid a very serious car accident. I was supposed to drive from Seattle to Olympia to visit a friend one afternoon, but I got the distinct feeling that a car accident was in my energy field. The feeling was clear enough that I called the pet sitter and left instructions on how to get in to feed the pets in case I didn't return from Olympia. I think I confused her somewhat because she didn't understand why I was telling her about how to get into my house; I omitted the part about an impending car accident because I didn't want to worry her. As I started on my journey, I felt into the energy of the car accident and located a crazy swirl of a pattern in my base chakra. I spent the entire trip down to Olympia untangling and sorting out that pattern. After the visit, I had pretty much forgotten about the pattern and headed home, arriving safely. After taking care of the pets, I decided I would head to another friend's house just a few miles away, as I had been invited over for the evening. I headed out, and then a weird series of events occurred.

I stopped at a stop sign at a Y-type intersection, and seeing that the lane I was to merge into was free, I headed into that lane. Oddly enough, I kept my eye on the car in the far lane of oncoming traffic which, I realized as I moved a bit forward, was travelling far too fast. The car then recklessly swerved into the lane I was merging into. I stopped, and the other driver saw my car, slammed on his brakes and went careening past me, lightly swiping my front bumper. He completely lost control of his car, did a full 180-degree spin, and slammed into a metal light post. With a blown out tire and smashed up car, the driver slowly pulled back into the street and headed off, not stopping at all!

I realized that if I had followed my usual driving habits, I would have been fully in front of that speeding, out of control vehicle. I was grateful that I had respected the feeling I had earlier in the day, enough to work on the pattern until it did little damage—a seventy-dollar fix at the body shop and my car was pretty much as good as new. We do draw these experiences toward us. So if I'm lucky enough to notice the pattern emerging in advance of the experience, then I pay attention and make the adjustments that will lead to a different experience.

I believe that once you trust yourself, you can completely trust your guides. As I mentioned earlier, I'm of the mind that I am tapping into some larger aspect of myself. Because of this, there really is no issue for me about whether the consciousness that is guiding me can be trusted. Of course, I trust myself! In fact, I believe that other humans are the ones we should be wary of, not our guides. Our beliefs about the powers of other humans can be more destructive than our guides will ever be!

THE GURU IS DEAD

Once you learn to trust yourself, you realize that the time is past to follow another unquestioningly. The way to personal power is increasingly up to you and your willingness to develop it. Working together and sharing knowledge is not what I'm speaking about here at all. When you are just setting forth on a conscious path, taking workshops or going to conferences can be invaluable, as others may be able to provide you with some shortcuts. In addition, gathering together to create more expansive states through field effects can also be useful to the process of gaining your own power. Learning from those who are further along the path or receiving grace from a guru is not necessarily a bad thing. The problem is when you give your power away.

While it may have been useful in the past to blindly follow the rules and biddings of someone acknowledged as being further along in their path, the time is quickly approaching where we must have our own powers fully sourced. Do you ask your mentor questions such as, "What should I do next? Where should I live? What career path should I follow?" If so, then you are giving away your power. A better question to ask is, "How can I tell which career path I should follow?" A great mentor will help you develop the skills you need to trust in your own power and discernment. If your mentor tells you that you can't trust yourself or your guides, and you need to check with him or her to make sure you don't screw up your spiritual path, then I would highly recommend running, not walking, in the opposite direction.

If you've found yourself in situations where you've given away your power to a mentor or teacher, then don't beat yourself up. I too have had these situations. Have I had teachers that exploited my trust? Yes. But always I remember that it takes two to tango. I can berate the teachers for being power-hungry, or for their own personal failings, but the situation only happens when I give away my power. Reclaiming your power is all that is needed. Move on along your path a little wiser. You are really the only person responsible for your path.

How can you tell if a teacher or mentor is one you should be learning from? Well, if I were to tell you that you don't know enough to choose your teachers, so you should check with me first, that would be a big red flag! Run! If the teacher says, "I cover that in my workshop next weekend, would you like to sign up?" Well, this is reasonable. It is more effective time-wise and energy-wise to share information with a group rather than with each person individually. And compensation for sharing what they know is not unreasonable either, even in matters of spirit. However, if the teacher says, "You must commit to my five-year program and tithe 50% of your income," that's a red flag. I don't care if this person can levitate and walk through walls, being his student is not going to move you more fully into your own power.

Also watch and learn from the way the teacher interacts with current students. Does the teacher celebrate the successes of the students? What happens when a student outperforms the teacher? A good teacher wants this to happen. The best teachers want their students to become colleagues, acknowledging that the student is there to teach the master as well. If your prospective teacher wants to take credit for the students' successes, or is competitive with rather than supportive of the advanced students, then I'd recommend treading carefully. And lastly, anyone can be a teacher. There are advanced beings doing great work on Earth, and connecting with them can benefit you. And even the most unlikely being can teach you much: the grocery clerk, the prisoner, or even the stray cat.

You can learn many awesome things from teachers and mentors—regardless of whether they are egoic or humble, competitive or supportive—as long as you don't give your power away. There is no need to throw the baby out with the bath water. You can take what is useful, but always use your own judgment. A good teacher may challenge you and your assumptions; in fact you should expect this, as this is how we learn! A good teacher may push you out of your comfort zone. But even if your teacher is right to do so, you need to keep your own sovereignty.

For example, I once had a mentor who told me something about myself that I didn't think was true. But I also believed she knew more than I did. So I floundered in a tough place. I could trust myself or I could trust my mentor. I tried to expand my assumptions; maybe I was wrong. But in the end, it still didn't feel right to me. So I made a choice. If I gave away my power and believed what she was saying was true, then I would be always wondering if I could trust myself. I had to choose to trust myself. Without this, I had nothing. I might be wrong, but I decided I would trust what felt right to me. Empowering myself was the right decision.

No one outside of yourself can know what is right for you, even if they have unerring clairvoyance. All things are really interpretations. If you choose yourself, and then later come to understand your mentor was right, then great! You didn't lose yourself in the process, which I believe is more important. Years later, I did see what my mentor had been talking about. But I also was aware that my mentor's interpretation was wrong and colored by her own biases. So in this situation, she was both right and wrong. I was ultimately glad I chose to honor myself instead of accepting her interpretation. I have, in fact, never regretted any decision to stay congruent with what feels right to me, even when I have learned later that I was mistaken.

This commitment to honor your self is the way you become your own guru. The question of right and wrong is far, far less important.

6

USING
CONSCIOUSNESS
TO CREATE HEALTH

Expansion of awareness and consciousness, for me, has been an amazing path for its own sake. But I didn't start out feeling that way at all! When I first began playing in the fields of consciousness, it wasn't because I wanted to become enlightened—not even close. In actuality, and I'm not too embarrassed to admit it, I began my pursuits because I saw other people doing magical things, and I wanted to be able to do magic too. You might say to me, "Well, you were training to be a healer. You must have wanted to learn these magical things in order to help others." I have to tell you outright, that you're mistaken. The main reason I wanted to heal people was so I could feel like an accomplished healer, not because of any altruistic idea of healing others or being of service. While I did think that being of service was a nice perk, I was very aware that I was pursuing the craft for my own ego fulfillment.

I am fairly certain that most healers begin their careers to help others. But, in the beginning, the desire to cure cancer may come strongly from the desire to be known as a cancer-curer, though it's great that the client gets a reprieve from their seemingly pending death sentence. The ego is at play big time when we first get into this field of expanding consciousness, whether we come to it as a healer or as a philosopher or as an artist. Your path always begins with ego.

The story I am about to tell, of the first time cancer mysteriously disappeared for a client, will show that there is nothing for the ego to claim, as this type of work can happen without you. The first time one of my clients went into remission with her cancer was completely accidental on my part! While she was cancer-free, I could not claim to be a cancer-curer.

The woman's daughter had come to me for a session, and at the end asked if there was anything I could do for her mother, who had had stage-four breast cancer. For four years she had taken all the normal medical courses of action, to no avail. While her daughter wanted her to pursue alternative treatments, her husband, fearful of losing his wife, wanted her to follow medical advice. The doctors had decided to put her in a trial with a new drug, but the possible side-effects could be harsh.

This was all I was told of the mother's situation. Cancer was serious, a big deal! I'd never worked with anything this serious before! I was pretty sure, due to my low self-esteem at the time, that I couldn't cure cancer. But I decided to use my meta-rule that my disbelief was not going to affect the results of the session. Since I didn't think I could do anything about cancer, I had the idea that perhaps I could shift the energy patterns enough that her final medical treatment could have the desired effect. I heard that voice in my head saying, *Sure . . . maybe . . . but then the medical doctors will get the credit for the results!* Seriously, could my ego be any more annoying? I was worried about who would get credit! I told that voice to back off. Who cares who gets credit if someone has a better chance at life?

I gathered the energetic patterns of the disease, of the family and their worries, and of the doctors and their treatments. I held the entire situation within my conscious awareness and watched it shift. That was it. That's all I did. I was hoping that now, since my thought had been to create a situation where the treatment would help her, she might get better results from the medical trial. Fortunately I always used the meta-rule that my left brain thoughts couldn't affect the results, because what happened next was completely unexpected.

A few days later, I received an email from the daughter. The doctors had called the family and told them that they had changed their mind about the treatment. They now had a new treatment which would not be as harsh on the physical body as the other option they had considered. The family, of course, was very happy with this. But it gets better. When the mother went in to do the pre-treatment work-up, the doctors discovered that there was nothing there to treat! The cancer had disappeared! It was amazing. And humbling. In that moment I realized very clearly, that I would never be known as a cancer-curer, or any other kind of healer. I may open the door for new possibilities, but I am not the one doing the work. Grace alone gets the credit here. I discovered that this is always the case with this kind of work. I cannot heal you, but together we can access a state of transformation for grace to step in.

The above example also shows that the trick to allowing shifts to happen in our own lives, and for our clients, is to not be too invested in the outcome. Darn that ego! It's going to find a way to limit us if it can! So when you first step into applying your expanded awareness to change the reality of yourself or others, you'll find the meta-rules I covered earlier indispensable. Think of whatever it is you want to change in your own life. Maybe you have allergies, back pain, or a lazy eye. Whatever seems to be less than ideal with your physical health is something you can practice with in this chapter. Start with whatever seems simplest to you. When I was first beginning, aches and pains seemed simpler to me. Cancer disappearing in your first attempt is possible, and yet building some momentum with your skills might be more important. If you don't heal cancer on the first try, don't give up and think you will never be able to do this! As we move through this chapter, laugh and have some fun. Approach this with the joy of learning and with your curiosity at full throttle, and you will progress quickly!

Over the years I've come to notice that healing is complex in that each individual is unique. I can't approach all clients in the same way, even if they have the same symptoms. There is much we could discuss here, but I want to keep this as simple as possible and share the few basic things you need to know that will apply to any situation. In alchemy, there are only three things you need to create transformation:

1. A container;
2. The thing you want to change—in our case it will be a pattern; and
3. The energy, or consciousness, to change it.

That's it!

THE ALCHEMICAL CONTAINER

The purpose of a container is to set aside space and time that is outside of the regular 3-D reality. We know that a normal waking state isn't the mindset we want to be in. Similarly, the normal rules of reality are not the rules we want to use when we are accessing transformation. A container does not need to be solid to separate a special space and time out of the typical reality we live in.

For my local clients, I have an office that can be used as a physical space marker. But many of my clients call me on the telephone and have their sessions from a distance. For them, the time frame we use can set the boundaries of the container. We have both set aside an hour of time to come together and transform. You can use anything as a container. I have used a tai-chi class as a container. I often use trips to distant locations as containers. I always use my workshops as a container. For example, if I have been feeling some fear holding me back from something I want to accomplish, I will set my intent that the pattern be shifted during the weekend workshop. The workshop acts as my container. All you need to decide is when and where the transformation will take place, and you have in effect cast a sacred circle, much like the magicians of long ago.

It's interesting to note that when ritual magicians would cast their circles, they would use a phrase that marked the space as being "between worlds." This is important because it means that the rules of the 3-D world we live in no longer apply. It is also an apt description of where consciousness moves when we are accessing the space of transformation. It is not an external space, but an internal one. The circle, office, or hour you have set aside becomes a representation of that internal world.

EVERYTHING EXISTS AS A PATTERN

What's needed next is the "thing" you want to change. Ancient alchemists used plants, minerals, and metals. Spiritual alchemists identify an aspect of personality that is holding them back or an energetic block in their field. You can choose the topic of your transformation, such as allergies or a back ache. But this is just the topic; the "thing" we want to change is the pattern that creates that symptom. Students often ask me why the pain returns after the session. They often find they are able to shift the energy pattern enough to have the pain go away, but later it returns. When I ask them what they were intending to change, they tell me that they wanted the pain to go away. But that may be too narrow in scope. Pain may be the topic here, but considering the underlying pattern, not the symptom of pain, may provide better results. There is such a thing as being too focused with your intent.

All things in the 3-D reality are produced from patterns of light and information; I prefer to look for these patterns that are creating the symptom in the 3-D world. To understand better how this happens, I like to use a model based on holographic principles. Once again, this model is useful to help us understand the concepts enough to access the change we want. However, I suspect that no model offers the full story, no matter how well it works. So use these concepts if they help you find the pattern you want to change.

HOLOGRAPHIC HEALING

When I work with clients, and look for the patterns that are creating something they want to change, I use a hologram as a conceptual model. Remember in *Star Wars*, R2D2 shines a 3-D projection of Princess Leia from a film he was a carrying. On the film is a pattern of information which does not look anything like the object that will appear in 3-D when a light shines through the film. How is this pattern recorded? Well, photons are passed over an object, resulting in interference patterns that create a sort of scrambling effect. These interference waves move back and forth and when they hit the film, they register as a pattern of information.

If you looked at the film, you would not see the snow man, or pebble, or apple that you passed the photon light across; you would just see a random pattern. But, when you shine a light through that film, you see the object projected into 3-D space. This was what R2D2 did to send Princess Leia's message to Obi Wan Kenobi. He sent light through a film which projected a 3-D hologram into space. Princess Leia repeated the same message over and over, because there was only one static pattern on the film.

We can use this idea by imagining that our 3-D world is like a holographic projection. With our consciousness, we can alter the patterns that are encoded on the film template. This model provides a basic conceptual model of how we can create our reality with just our consciousness, which I have found very useful! When I speak of holographic healing, I mean that the shifts in our reality occur because we change this pattern of light and information that is encoded in a space just beyond the 3-D reality.

Many people refer to this space by different names. You may have heard terms like zero-point field, quantum field of possibilities, the void, or even the ancient alchemical term, "first matter." What you call the space that contains the patterns of light and information is less important than having a conceptual model that works for you. In the Holographic Healing model, we will access this field of possibilities with our consciousness, which is why the consciousness-expanding exercises from the first part of this book are so important.

If the patterns of light and information stay static, then we get a repeating experience in the 3-D world, similar to Princess Leia repeating her message. If our experiences seem stuck in our 3-D reality, we can use the Holographic Healing model to make changes and upgrades to that pattern of light and information. Thus, when we pop into this 3-D reality, we have a different experience than what we were having before we changed the template. Physicists have begun to create their own models to explain this space containing the patterns of light and information. It's not crucial that you understand the complexities of the scientific models to use this system. But for those of you who are interested in delving deeper into the science, I have set up a resources page on my website to support you in that endeavor.

Quite simply, when I refer to patterns, I am referring to a complex interference pattern of information which does not exist in the 3-D reality. We can't find these patterns in the material world. This is why we spent the first part of the book working on moving our awareness. Consciousness can access these patterns because it can go to places our physical body cannot. Even more simply, just beyond the border of physical reality lay patterns of information that eventually pop into our 3-D reality. Our human physicality exists in the 3-D world, but that physical body is being informed by patterns of light and information that lie beyond 3-D reality. When we access these patterns directly, we are reaching beyond our human selves into an infinite play of possibilities! We can access these patterns and possibilities and shape them to create new realities in our 3-D world.

Your conception of what patterns might look like is probably just as good as mine. For me, the information runs in grid lines. Patterns and tangles get created when that information gets disrupted or damaged. So to change the discomfort of pain, for example, I would be searching with my awareness for the pattern that creates that discomfort. The pattern creating the pain is what we want to work with, not the pain itself.

THE BASICS OF FINDING A PATTERN

Numerous ways to access patterns can be found. Once you've gotten out of your head and into your heart, your ability to notice information is amplified. All you are doing here is noticing information. You can see a pattern, feel a pattern, hear a pattern, or simply know that you are connected to it. Anyway you notice is absolutely right for you. So explore and experiment until you decide how things occur for you when you are dipping your consciousness into this world of patterns.

Personally, since I am lazy, I prefer the pattern to come to me, to simply arrive in my awareness. I also like to "hold" it in my hand. If I know someone has back pain, I ask for the pattern related to that pain to show up in my hand. If this seems confusing to you, you can assign the pattern to something else. For example, you can hold a banana in your hand (or a pillow or a doll) and simply decide that the object will represent the pattern. Yes, in this special sacred container that you have created for transformation, anything can represent anything else, if you say so. Those who are more visual may prefer to see a pattern floating in front of them.

One of the biggest stumbling blocks at this point is to believe that someone's back should represent their back pain. In truth, you want to be able to see far beyond physical reality to access the light and information behind it. You are not changing someone's back in this example. You are changing the pattern of information that is showing up as the experience of back pain. You are moving beyond the human body into the patterns that create the physical body with your conscious awareness. Remember the child in The Matrix who knowingly says, "You must realize the truth. That there is no spoon." Once you get that down, allowing for the pattern to emerge will come more and more naturally. If you find this difficult, simply practice—with anything and everything! The "Finding Patterns" exercise explains the basics for noticing patterns.

EXERCISE

Finding Patterns

- Hold an object, such as an apple, in your hand. Or rest it on a table near you.

- Use any of the previous exercises that move your awareness out of your head.

- Allow your awareness to sink into your heart-space.

- Ask for the pattern of the apple to show up. Be aware of any type of information: a visual cue, a feeling, a weight, a knowing. For me, frequently a pattern looks like a jumbled ball of yarn that shows up in my hand. You might see swirls of colors if you're visual. You might hear a buzz if you are auditory. Or perhaps you feel a hard spot in the field. Abstract representations are often ideal, as a more concrete image can move us back into our heads to critique or interpret it, which we should avoid if we can.

- Try the exercise with a number of different objects, simply noticing what you become aware of.

CONSCIOUSNESS AND INTENT

Once we have identified a pattern, we are going to want to change it. The whole point is to create a different experience. An alchemist needs energy to create transformation. I suggest that consciousness is the energy you seek. Pure consciousness is a divine energy source and is all you need to create all manner of transformation in the 3-D physical world. Your awareness accessed from your heart field is a doorway to unlimited possibility!

One tip for creating the change you seek is to not be very specific about what needs to happen with the pattern you discover. You may have heard just the opposite, as many people teach manifestation by telling you to be very specific about what you want. I, on the other hand, find that specificity tends to limit the way the pattern can shift.

In the beginning it is common to be too specific—focusing on making the pain go away or making the cancer disappear. Or, if the problem is that our partner is ignoring us, we decide exactly how his or her behavior should be. It doesn't take very long, going down this path, to realize that we may be on shaky ground deciding exactly how something should change. Can we really take into consideration every factor in order to know what is right? We often lament about something sad happening and wish we didn't have to experience it. But later we realize that this very experience was responsible for bringing terrific new opportunities, and we end up happier than we ever were before!

Originally, ritual magicians would do a divination before they attempted to create the magical change they wanted. This divination was a way of asking the universe if this change would be right to do. Would this be of benefit to all? A few years ago, a television show called *Pushing Daisies* illustrated this dilemma beautifully. The main character learns he can bring dead things back to life. A bird flies into a window and dies, but when he touches the bird, it springs back to life! But what he doesn't know, at first, is that as the bird came to life, a squirrel died in the neighboring tree. That's an extreme example, but it is a wise person who knows that just because you can do something, doesn't mean you should. I, for one, have no idea what the best outcome could be for a person. In any moment we have limited knowledge, so judging what would be better for someone is simply not possible.

An old Sufi tale teaches of the dangers of trying to judge what is good or bad. The tale begins with a farmer whose son has returned home, having captured a strong wild horse. "How fortunate," his neighbors exclaim. "We will see," the farmer replies. The next week, the farmer's son is thrown from the horse, breaking his leg. "How horrible! What misfortune! What a curse!" his neighbors cry. "We will see," the farmer replies. The following week, soldiers come and take all the able-bodied men from the village to fight in the army. The farmer's son remains behind with his injury. "How fortunate you are," declare the neighbors. And the farmer patiently replies, "We will see." The story has always reminded me that instant healing may not always be the most useful outcome. We cannot know what lies ahead.

When I was a novice healer, I was not so concerned that someone's instantaneous healing might be detrimental, but I was really scared that I might make a client worse. Of course, "worse" is as much of a judgment as "better." But, I wasn't very clear on how any of this worked, and I really didn't want to do something that might harm someone out of my own ignorance. So I created the meta-rule that I could only get two kinds of results: either the change would be more useful, or nothing at all would happen. If nothing happened, that would be the universe's way of saying that it shouldn't. Although it can be frustrating as a results-oriented person to have nothing happen, I was okay with that, as it also meant I wasn't going to screw someone up.

I also didn't always know what a better outcome might be. I used to think I needed to know what the healthy, pain-free shoulder would look like. I spent weeks pouring over anatomy and physiology books, and always had them on hand to reference when a client showed up. While there is nothing wrong with this approach, it's not necessary. So what can I do instead? Usually I just hold space for something to change. I do not direct it on how to change. There is an innate intelligence greater than my small mind that knows far better than I ever could what something more useful might look like. I trust that. And I have noticed that when my awareness touches a pattern, and I hold an expectation for something to change, the pattern simply begins to change. I don't have to know how it should change, and I don't have to direct it.

CALIBRATION OF RESULTS

Once you have noticed that the pattern changed, then you can look for the change in the experience or symptom in the 3-D reality. It is important to remember that you do not need to get rid of the pattern you are observing. Many of us have models that we need to remove bad programming or clear energies that are harming us. In the holographic model, the pattern you are observing does not need to be removed or disappear entirely for the shift to occur. Once you've shifted anything in that pattern, you have a new pattern of light and information, and what you experience in the 3-D reality is going to be different. Period.

The new experience is also made up of patterns of light and information. What I look for when observing a pattern is that it appears more harmonious, less distorted, untangled, or I simply feel a sense of peace and calm when observing it. Often, either I or the client or both will experience a yawn or deep breath, which for me indicates a good shift in the pattern. So anything that shifts, moves or changes means that the pattern is different. Even the tiniest little shift can equal a huge difference in experience.

EXERCISE

Changing a Health Pattern

* Decide on the topic, such as back pain or allergies.

* Allow your awareness to move out of your head and into your heart-space.

* Ask the pattern that is creating your topic to emerge.

* Notice that pattern however it shows up, letting go of your expectations of how you think it should look.

* As you observe it, simply touch your awareness to the pattern. If it doesn't immediately begin to change in your awareness, then you can suggest a change. Often a simple question, "Would you like to change?" is enough.

* End the session, and then notice what seems different

with your topic. Does the pain feel different? Does anything else in your experience seem different?

Anything can indicate that you or your client is different. Once I noticed that I didn't like pizza anymore, even though it had been my favorite food. Clients have sometimes reported that people interact with them differently after a session. Others say that they have more neutral emotional reactions to issues that used to really upset them. All of these are important indicators that the pattern is different. So stay alert for all the indications that you have achieved a result, and don't limit yourself to only observing if the pain has changed.

What I've described in the "Changing a Health Pattern" exercise are the most basic principles to assist healing with only your consciousness. This alchemical formula really is as simple and easy to use as I describe. However, I remember my early days of studying these ancient healing methods. I did not believe it could be so simple! I was sure that I wasn't doing it right, and I focused on anything that looked like failure. By doing so, I entirely missed all the miracles that were happening. A great example of this was a student who had just learned a new technique. She applied it with her nephew who suffered from eczema. The next day, the eczema was gone from one half of his body! She asked me, in all seriousness, "What did I do wrong?" The only thing she did wrong was fail to recognize what a huge and amazing shift she created!

Tapping into grace and creating miracles is very simple if you use this model. And yes, you can add layers and permutations and create all kinds of methods and procedures to make the process more exciting and interesting to you. I did just that as I was learning. Making it more complicated appeased my left brain and made me feel like I was doing something during the sessions. But eventually I came back to the simple, basic, pure awareness of patterns and the state of transformation. It is a method I have been working with for many years.

7

USING
CONSCIOUSNESS
TO CREATE
FINANCIAL FREEDOM

Once we have a basic framework for making changes, we can use it for anything. Remember, everything is a pattern, even money. Helping with money issues is one of the most popular requests I receive in my practice, second perhaps only to health issues. Money is, in our culture especially, a really hot topic. When we begin to realize that consciousness has the ability to shift our 3-D reality, it is not unusual for thoughts to turn quickly to winning the lottery, generating an endless supply of clients with no effort, or even manifesting huge piles of cash which magically appear on the coffee table any time we desire. I can certainly relate to wanting to manifest these desires.

CREATING AN IMMEDIATE SHIFT

Okay. Let's start where we are. Here we sit in our 3-D reality, experiencing whatever financial situation we are currently in. Maybe some of us have lost jobs, maybe we have lost a house recently, or maybe we have had to cut back on our entertainment. Maybe we are anticipating additional expenses due to holidays or birthdays coming up. Maybe an unexpected expense has occurred, with the roof leaking or the car breaking down. Maybe we are always uncertain about how the bills will get paid by the end of the month. We need a higher-paying job, or an inheritance, or some clients to call, or we need a judgment to finally be paid. We're waiting on money to come our way.

You may notice that thinking about these things makes you quite tense, with muscles tightening as you consider your current circumstances. One of the first things you can do to improve your experience in 3-D and to create some leverage for changing it, is to relax. You can continue to think about the situation, but you consciously relax your body and all the tight places. Go ahead and do that. Already your experience is improved. In this moment, with the same situation, you are more relaxed, you are less tense, and your living experience is better. The first tip, then, is this: Every time you feel yourself tense up as you think of a money situation, direct yourself to relax. This contradiction of habit will make the patterns you have around money more malleable and easier to shift.

SEEING YOUR PATTERNS

Now that you are more relaxed, I'd like you to come with me on a short visualization. The goal of the exercise "Shifting

Your Money Patterns" is to allow an abstract representation of your relationship to finances to present itself. If you are not someone who easily visualizes, you can still use this exercise; perhaps you will touch or feel the pattern or use another type of awareness. For me, the easiest way to see a pattern is to imagine a tangled ball of yarn. It might be many colors or one color. It might be loosely tangled or tightly tangled. It might have areas of relative order and other spots of tangled mess. This is just a representation of information, and there is no need to judge it or understand it in order to begin to see it change. This is why this task can be so easy—as long as you keep your thinking mind, which wants to interpret and understand, out of it!

EXERCISE

Shifting Your Money Patterns

- Move your awareness out of your head into the heart-space of transformation.

- As in the previous chapter, when we worked with health, ask for the pattern of your relationship with money to present itself in front of you. This pattern will include all aspects of yourself that relate to finances: feelings of unworthiness, ingrained beliefs from your parents or family, past life associations, ancestral influences, cultural expectations, as well as anything else that is related. The nice thing here is that you do not need to understand what is included in the pattern. It is wise not to read too much into the image and how it represents the relationship.

* Again, remember to relax everything that is tight in your body as you watch this pattern.

* Now watch how it begins to change. Sometimes you may simply see the change happen while you watch, while other times you may feel an inclination to inter-act with the pattern. Perhaps you notice that one side is more tangled, in which case you can reach in with your awareness to unwind the threads.

* Take a few moments and just watch how this pattern changes.

* Once you've noticed something about the pattern change, then you're done!

Really, that's it! Don't assume because the pattern is still there you'll still have problems! Many people believe that they must eliminate the pattern, but they are incorrect. Don't assume that a pattern is something negative. Even the people who have a good relationship to finances, still have a pattern! The changes you observed may be all you need for a pattern to shift from something not useful to something very useful indeed! You don't need to keep doing the visualiza-tion every day. Simply look for ways that your relationship to money seems different.

❖ ❖ ❖

THE POWER OF GRATITUDE

You hear many people advocate that gratitude helps attract abundance. While I agree with this idea in principle, I often see people practice it somewhat falsely. This idea that if I say I'm grateful, I'll get the stuff I want, is not useful. It's like a four-year old apologizing, not because he is sorry, but because he can't have dessert if he doesn't. If you practice gratitude only so you can get stuff, then you're not doing it right! And likely you will find gratitude of very little use to you.

I found out about the power of gratitude quite accidentally. I had heard about the concept, and I got to wondering . . . *What is gratitude? What does it feel like?* I wasn't certain that I had the right idea of what gratitude was and I was very curious. Now, at this point in my life, I had a teaching job that was contracted quarter to quarter. I netted maybe $1,700–$1,800 each month, in a city with a pretty high cost of living. I had no savings to speak of. I did own a car, but I did not have television or internet. I had never set foot inside Nordstrom's as I bought clothing only in second hand stores. It was a month to month existence. However, I never felt that I went without. I felt that I was lucky, as I truly had everything I needed. I had learned that most of what Americans considered as necessities were actually quite optional. I practiced what I came to refer to as smart money managing, paying close attention to avoid extraneous fees and things like that. So even though I didn't have much, I didn't really feel deprived of anything. This attitude very likely worked in my favor, since I wasn't attached to any specific outcome.

At the time I became curious about gratitude, I had begun

my healing practice and had a few clients. However, I had been passed over for a contract for summer teaching work, so I would basically be unemployed for the summer. I also had hoped to visit Peru the following year, but knew I would need to create the means to do that. That was my financial situation then, but I didn't really have a goal to change any of that specifically. Instead, I just wanted to explore this idea of gratitude and figure out what that was. So I began a gratitude meditation sitting with my coffee in the backyard garden, which had the unexpected side-effect of significantly improving my financial situation. You can do the exercise "Gratitude Meditation" and discover your own hidden gifts.

EXERCISE

Gratitude Meditation

♦ Get quiet. Close your eyes and relax.

♦ Ask for the feeling of gratitude to show up in your body. Notice what happens.

♦ If you feel nothing, just wait and be a little patient. Maybe you feel just a slight twinge somewhere, or a bit of warmth, or maybe a little pressure or movement.

♦ Whatever the feeling is, don't discount it. Just move your awareness to it. When I first began, I originally felt just a small feeling in my chest. Very small.

♦ If you have only a slight feeling, ask for the feeling to amplify: ten times, 100 times, 1000 times, etc.

• Simply sit in the feeling. Notice that each time you do
the meditation, the feeling grows and amplifies.

As I did this meditation daily, I noticed that gratitude was
an amazing and blissful feeling. The feeling of gratitude was so
awesome, that when I was in it, I was very clear that I needed
nothing else. In the center of gratitude I was everything and
had everything anyone could ever want. When you have this
realization, you quickly understand that you do not need to
chase money, you need only chase gratitude. Gratitude is truly
all you need.

As I continued the gratitude meditation, I noticed quite
accidentally that positive changes were happening in my everyday life. Out of the blue I received a package from a client. I was
afraid to open it, as I felt I had not helped him very much. A
part of me was sure he had mailed me rocks from the volcano
near his Hawaiian home! But when I finally opened the package,
it was stuffed full of Hawaiian gifts and food and a twenty dol-
lar bill! Then I moved to a new house share, which was cheaper
than where I had been living. I calculated that the savings over
the year at this new home would equal the amount I needed to
go to Peru! Then a friend asked me to housesit her home and
dog in California near the beach—a free vacation! I accepted,
and then received a call from the school. They had a class for me
to teach because a faculty member had become ill—and it just
happened to be an online class, so I could do it from California!
The amount I'd be paid for the class would also pay for the trip

to Peru, so I had doubled the amount I needed with no effort at all. I also decided I would see come clients while in California, since I had some contacts there. Well, I barely got to vacation at all, as people were very eager to book appointments since I would only be there for a limited time!

I came to understand that when you spend time vibrating in gratitude, you attract experiences of the same vibration. However, even when you are vibrating in gratitude daily, you may have an unfortunate experience or two. While I was in California, I ended up in the ER twice, and one of my cats back home died. However, I was peaceful. I was not stressed and distraught about these events at all. I felt sadness at my cat's passing, but I was okay. Sometimes, people latch on to a negative experience as evidence that their gratitude meditation or healing session didn't work. But a better perspective might be to examine how you are responding to the glitches when they occur. I may have had a health glitch or two and experienced some grief at losing my cat, but I was able to move in the flow with life easily—despite all of life's ups and downs. Being in such a state of grace allowed me to evenly navigate the hiccups without any undue stress! This was new, since in the past these types of experiences had always thrown me into a lot of emotional stress. I won't claim that practicing gratitude means everything will always go your way, but I still highly recommend it because it can radically change your response to stressful situations!

Indeed, the true gift of practicing the gratitude meditation the way I did it back then was that I came to understand that we always have everything we need, we are always whole and complete. Experiencing gratitude so profoundly, allowed me to let go of the idea that I lacked anything. I was no longer looking at my life in terms of what I lacked. This shift in perspective is the key to creating wondrous things. But it goes counter to the ego that pursues this concept because it wants something. That is okay, though. We have to go easy on our ego, as often it is the reason we venture in this direction at all.

THE MORPHIC FIELD OF MONEY

Let's consider another aspect of the financial freedom game— the aspects of the game that are larger than our individual selves. While we can control our sense of gratitude and many of our own specific patterns, the morphic field of the economic system extends beyond our complete control. When it comes to the financial markets and economies, the morphic field is global. We are not only affected by the country we reside in but also by things that happen elsewhere which cause shifts in the morphic field. As you can imagine, these larger fields can act as an imprint, affecting your individual vibration in these matters. Yes, your money problems might not be your problems at all! The mood of the nation affects you, and influences greatly your sense of possibility. You may work on yourself, but the larger morphic fields can hamper the shifting that you've done with your own patterns in relationship to money.

In 2008, as banks were failing and people worried about economic collapse, my friends and acquaintances were all concerned about how this would affect them. Friends, relatives, and clients, would all tell stories of a friend's nephew getting laid off or of hearing on the news of people losing their jobs. They considered their fields of employment, the industries they were involved in, and whether they needed to make changes to their lifestyles or future plans. Over and over again they would tell me that my business would certainly suffer because in hard times, woo-woo things such as energy healing were not an essential expense. Despite their concern, I didn't spend much time thinking about what might happen to my business. My thoughts were kept busy with my current clients and activities.

After a couple of months of this, I was sitting at my office, having just finished working with clients for the day. I allowed my thoughts to drift into the future. I could feel the economy sinking as if it were an anchor, and I watched as my business began to tilt with it. *Oh*, I thought. *That won't do. I should do something to change that!* And so I noticed where my business was linked to this larger morphic field labeled "economy," and I just separated the two out. I let the larger economy field, which was acting like an anchor for my business, slip away and out of sight. I noticed my business float off in a different direction. Basically I did what I showed you in the first exercise, but with *two* interrelated patterns: the larger morphic field and the smaller pattern of my business. What happened then was a steady climb in revenues for my business, the opposite of the economy's performance. And that was it. That was all I did. I did not change how I ran or approached my business. I continued to make business decisions based on my guidance, as I had before.

EXERCISE

Detaching from Morphic Fields

You can either look at your business in relation to the larger morphic field, or you can look at your family unit's economy if you don't run your own business. The family unit is like a business, yes?

• Drop your awareness out of your head so you're looking with all of your greater senses.

• Ask for the larger morphic pattern to show up. How does the morphic field of the nation's economy look to you? And again, if you don't visualize, then you can notice what it feels like.

• Now imagine where the pattern representing your business or family economy is in relation to the larger morphic field.

• Notice what happens next. Does the shift happen on its own? Or do you need to untangle the two patterns?

• Continue watching until you feel that the connections are all severed, and your business or family pattern is separate and distinct from the morphic field.

Do realize that separating from the morphic field may be advantageous in a down economy, but you may want entanglement when the economy is moving in a positive direction.

Planetary morphic fields may be useful or not, so don't assume that you must always untangle yourself. In addition, you can find morphic fields that you'd like to entangle with, and the next section will discuss just that!

FINDING ALTERNATIVES

There are many beliefs and structures that contribute to our struggles around money. We discuss some strategies for working with these in this chapter. However, if your only goal in reading this section is to learn how to generate large wads of cash, you might be successful, but you'll be missing the real gold, if you'll pardon the pun. There is a much larger issue at hand—true freedom, which comes from detachment from the entire current financial structure. When we ask to win the lottery or create a large number of paying customers, we are still engaging within the current structure. While it may be worth spending some time cleaning up your engagement with the current structure, playing outside the current financial structure may offer far bigger payoffs and immense freedom.

One of the challenges with this whole topic, is that it can be very difficult to imagine a life without money. We are enmeshed in a system that we don't want to be in, and at the same time we are at a loss to envision another system. For example, I may have money in an IRA, which relies on the current financial system to multiply and provide enough income for retirement. In this case I have banked my future on the continuation of the current system. I am also stuck in the belief that to retire, I need this IRA, and I can't imagine how things could be different. Being able to access new possibilities, even if we don't know what they are, is vitally important if we want to be truly financially free.

We need to consider how we can find alternatives to participate in. What would a new economy look like? I have difficulty envisioning something for which I have no previous reference point. An economy that is based on integrity, and values leisure time, creativity, and relationships—rather than the bottom line—seems like a unicorn. Does it exist? What would it look like in practical terms? Would we still have banks? What about corporations? What would my own business look like? Would I give things away for free?

Truly, developing an alternative for the current economy might be a long process, rather than a one-sweep-and-it's-complete scenario. But if only we could envision the new world, it would be easier to create! Well, not necessarily so. We can tap into ideas or new morphic fields that have not yet emerged into our conscious awareness. There are two important strategies that I often use to tap into things that are beyond my imagination. Incredibly useful tools for a myriad of situations, these are skills well worth practicing, as I have not yet met someone who hasn't gotten stuck in this place where the alternative is unimaginable.

Both tools are simple and easy to use. Try both and see what happens when you apply these in your world. Can't imagine what a healthy relationship looks like? Have no idea what it would be like to truly love yourself? These are the go-to tools for situations like these.

EXERCISE

Finding a New Option

This tool works best when you don't really like any of the options you can picture.

♦ First, draw yourself into the present moment and into your heart-space.

♦ Think about each of the possible options you are aware of for your situation.

♦ Place these options in each hand. If there are more than two options, imagine them in a semicircle around you.

♦ When you recognize that no options seem right, extend a "third" hand out from the center of your heart area.

♦ Ask the universe to drop a perfect solution or option into this hand.

♦ Notice what it feels like as the universe fills in this empty option.

You may or may not have an intellectual understanding of what was delivered to this third hand, but it doesn't matter during the exercise. The goal is to allow the energy of the new and best option to arrive. The details will reveal themselves as you move forward. Often a new inspiration or understanding will arrive in some form.

❖ ❖ ❖

EXERCISE

Moving beyond
Your Circle of Awareness

• First gather yourself into the present moment.

• Imagine that there is a circle around you, and you are perfectly in the center. This circle represents the domain of your awareness. All that you are presently aware of, and all that you know which is not presently in your awareness, exist inside this circle.

• You know that the answer you seek does not reside anywhere within this circle. Beyond the circle are all the things that you are not yet aware of.

• Move your awareness to the very edge of the circle.

• Take a finger of your awareness, and dip it into the field beyond the circle, with the intention of accessing the solution that is beyond your imagination.

• Notice what happens and what it feels like to have tapped into this new information.

Again, it is not important if you intellectually understand the information you've tapped into, though sometimes either one of these exercises will give you a sudden "aha!" moment of understanding. More importantly, you've tapped into the energy and patterns of the new thing that you are becoming or are bringing into the world. Now you simply notice what happens in your own world and leave all preconceived notions about what something should look like or be like aside.

As you play with these tools you will find that not knowing what the solution should be can lead to some pretty amazing outcomes. Many clients come to me asking to help their house sell quickly. When I ask them why they need their house to sell quickly, it often turns out that they need cash for some other endeavor. I then ask them if it would be okay for the resources for the new endeavor to show up any way the universe wants to send them. In my experience, the universe has some really unique solutions that I would have never thought of myself!

One of my clients, for example, needed a source of money, because her current assets were tied up in a contract that meant she could not access them for some time. So she was looking for new ways that money could flow into her life. Neither of us had any idea what the new sources of money could be, but we did the session anyway, using the tools I've shared in this chapter. The next thing I heard from her was truly miraculous! She retrieved the documents of the contract that was tying up her assets, and strangely, the date printed on them was months earlier than it had been on the original document. The ink itself that marked the new day looked fresher and newer. We have no idea how the universe changed the dates of her paperwork, but the result was that she now had access to her assets in a time frame that was going to work for her! Now, there is no way I would have ever thought to try to change the dates on paperwork! But thankfully, I don't have to know what the solution will be to access the possibility of a better outcome!

8

USING CONSCIOUSNESS TO CREATE GREAT RELATIONSHIPS

Got love? Are you wondering whether this simple process of shifting your life with conscious awareness is going to allow you to create the perfect soul mate? When it comes to working with other people, you can help others with their own healing or their relationship with money, but can you make them fall in love with you? If you're thinking about manipulating the perfect man or woman into love and marriage, you will be quite disappointed. But if you are willing to change yourself, you will find that relationships naturally improve and it is completely possible for you to attract love into your life. You are perhaps beginning to see that the process of transformation with just your conscious awareness can improve many areas of your life.

You may have heard that before someone else can love you, you have to love yourself. But what does that mean? I use one basic question to calibrate how my relationship to my Self is doing. I ask, "How safe am I?" I have experienced times when I have been so connected to my Higher Self and Source, that when my 3-D reality glitched a bit, I still felt okay. When unusual things occur it doesn't freak me out if my relationship to Self is solid. Nor do I get rattled by the myriad of things in the 3-D world that can make life tougher. Being able to feel strongly connected to Source when unexpected things happen is crucial in the game of consciousness. This ability is important because we all want to see *big* changes happen quickly now! To be able to deal with big changes, we must be completely connected to Source. I have been so solidly in this space of connection at times that I have felt that, if I woke up tomorrow in a foreign place without the ability to speak the language and with no idea of where I was or how I got there, I would still feel safe.

This realization that I could feel safe no matter what was happening was huge for me, because I was never a very adventurous person. I didn't like spur of the moment events because I needed to feel in control, even if that control was largely an illusion. However the advantage of being *that* connected to Self and Source is that you find yourself in a completely reliable and trustable position. There is nothing else that can provide that level of safety. Once you are fully sourced, you know that you are always safe, and the 3-D surroundings are inconsequential. This is why we need to focus on ourselves when considering any relationship—because we go to relationships for things such as safety, and then we are devastated when that safety proves false. The only way to have deep satisfying relationships is when you don't need them for safety. So let's separate the idea of relationship from the idea of safety from the start.

To have the most fun in the area of personal relationships, the connection to Self and individual power needs to be solid. If it is not, you end up at the whim of other forces: cultural, ancestral, childhood patterns, etc. It's never just about you and your partner; all relationships include the patterns of the woman's relationship to her mother, or the man's relationship to his father, for example. These patterns are forces that can be extremely strong and powerful. It is likely that even with a solid connection to Self and Source, you will still see these other powerful influences hold sway at times in your relationship to others.

What many of us do in our search for love and companionship is push our own energy outside of ourselves to search for the "other," the one who will fulfill us or engage us in companionship or perhaps just entertain us. Constantly searching outside ourselves can be a way of avoiding connecting with ourselves. You can see this with people who are constantly on the go—visiting every party, playing every sport, constantly finding something to do or people to distract them. I've certainly gone through this stage, and can remember how uncomfortable it was to be alone with myself. I slowly cultivated a practice of it, and now can even find myself spending too much time in this inward space! So if being in this inward space is new to you, go slow; but I guarantee that connecting to Source will help you create truly satisfying and fun relationships.

CONNECTING TO SOURCE

How does connecting to Source help you create better relationships? Here's an example. Let's say you want to manifest a partner or soul mate. This is a common request that people come to sessions with. The more you push outside of yourself to find someone to ease the loneliness or boredom or even to just share your thoughts with, the more you will notice that you feel lonely, bored, or bothered by not having another to share with. *The act of looking outside yourself, actually creates the emptiness.* Always, the trick to manifesting is not needing the thing you want to manifest. I know, such a paradox! By not needing, you must be in the energy of already having it. Be completely fulfilled and content, and you are more likely to manifest a partner or close friends.

Use the "Completing Your Own Circuits" exercise several times a day to create the conditions in yourself of already having everything you need. It is such a useful exercise that I recommend using it before making decisions and before drawing conclusions in the 3-D world. This exercise creates a bridge into new ways of being. With this, we can create the new structures—the new patterns on our holographic templates—that will move us beyond what we believe is possible for human potential. Indeed, since this is the power of love, this exercise can make you a master of love. But be ready to let go of much of what you thought was true about yourself, about others, and about relationships. When I practice this exercise, I notice that I feel first that I am getting filled up and then expanding. As I expand I feel that I am simply existing inside of unconditional love. It is such a great feeling, really!

EXERCISE

Completing Your Own Circuits

This exercise is an excellent one to help you do for yourself the one thing you've been searching to gain from others: to feel completely loved and completely safe in the world.

- First, bring yourself in from your day and become calm and centered.

- Take a few deep breaths and drop your awareness out of your head.

- Now become aware of the excitement you feel when thinking of being with your perfect companion. Perhaps you feel curiosity or deep connection or even deep love from having a fully present companion.

- Notice this feeling of excitement moving out through your heart into the world.

- Now imagine a copy of yourself, sitting across from you, facing you.

- Watch that stream of excitement connect and flow into the heart of your copy.

- Now, move your awareness until you inhabit the awareness of the copy who is receiving all your deep love.

- Notice how it feels to be your own beloved!

- Continue to receive the outpouring from the self that is opposite of you.

• Notice how you become filled up and overflowing from being your own beloved and receiving your own love!

This is a space of fullness that you want to create every day for yourself before you move out into the world. And when you do move out into the world, you want to be moving from this space. Once you are sitting in this amazing feeling, notice that when you think about having a soul mate the idea is not charged with negative angst, longing, or loneliness; instead, it feels neutral. You feel so good, you don't feel that you are missing anything! Now, do you think, based on what you know about the Law of Attraction, that it might be easier to attract a soul mate from this place rather than from a place of loneliness? And the great news is that even if you don't create the relationship right away, are you likely to even care? From this space, all of the stories you tell yourself—that you are lost, left behind, abandoned, unworthy—none of these are true and none of them hold sway.

From this beautiful expanded space, you can go further and make changes in the patterns that are plaguing your relationships. "The Mirror" exercise is equally effective for all relationships: boss, a parent, child, or even a friend. So think about all your relationships—not just the one with your significant other—when you think about shifting the patterns. Notice that one very important key in this exercise is that you are not changing the other person at all. You are only changing yourself; that is the most powerful change you can make in any relationship! In this exercise, the other person is only acting as a mirror, so you can find the patterns in yourself to change.

EXERCISE

The Mirror

- Think of someone who generally irritates you or with whom you experience problems.

- Do the "Completing Your Own Circuits" exercise.

- From here, check in—what part of you is attached to the drama or trauma here? Don't psychoanalyze, just let the pattern emerge.

- You can feel the pattern or visualize it, but try to stay clear of labeling or pinpointing a cause. Just let it be a pattern.

- Now you may observe that the pattern is already changing. Or you may decide to interact with the pattern with your awareness, unraveling it or untangling it. You might notice it fade or float. If you are feeling the pattern rather than visualizing it, then feel the dissipation. Decide it will shift and be confident that it will change because you decided it will.

- Calibrate the result by imagining the person who irritates you. How does the attachment to the drama or trauma feel now? Most people will notice a difference, and any difference means that it can continue to change if you decide it will.

• Calibrate the result in real time. Next time you see the person, notice if the irritation has changed. And if you do not notice a difference, then do the Completing the Circuits exercise right then, and notice if you still feel the same way.

These exercises are designed to allow you access to your own power of creation. They can work well for you in shifting your relationships, as well as in other areas of your life. Notice that "The Mirror" exercise is the basic exercise I used to shift my stolen-cat experience into a lost-cat experience. As you get comfortable with the exercises, feel free to experiment with them. If you wonder if they will work for a certain situation, simply try them and see. Remember, that you are the explorer of your consciousness. How you create your world is always unique to you. Modifying and changing the exercises to better fit you is perfectly acceptable and even encouraged.

SHIFTING THE PATTERNS
THAT HOLD US BACK FROM LOVE

Although the above exercises will help you improve any relationship, many clients come to me wondering why they have never experienced a deep and lasting love with a soul mate. Indeed, many people report a sense of being cut off from love in some very frustrating ways.

One woman, for example, told me that she will rage for weeks when she learns that someone has not told her the truth. She also goes into hysterics about how this person can never be trusted, and how *dare* he hurt her like that! Another friend confided that she never feels that she fits in and this causes her much anguish. She points to the fact that she was an Asian child adopted by white parents, so no matter how well her parents provided emotionally, it was never enough. Hmmm. . . . This is strange, as I wasn't adopted and had two perfectly normal parents, and yet I too never felt that I fit in. I was the odd duck in my family.

These experiences seem to be universal, as one friend—a man with an amazing soul who loves everyone and is loved dearly by everyone he meets—confided to me that he often feels disconnected and that others don't fully accept him! Therapists go to great lengths to pinpoint a childhood trauma that is the cause of these feelings. However, after listening to countless clients over the years, I have found that if you are human you will have patterns like these come into play in your life, no matter how perfect your childhood was. It is, indeed, the nature of the game we are playing here, so give yourself a break. Realize that maybe, just maybe, the *why* of this feeling is of little importance. Once you have tools to shift any pattern, you can let go of the stories around why it all came to be, and simply notice how different it can be in the next moment.

EXERCISE

Changing the Patterns that Keep You from Love

The key to this exercise is to let go of your judging mind. Don't assume you know why a pattern is there.

- Choose an experience you have noticed occurring for you repeatedly, such as "I always get upset when someone has not told me the truth."

- Then drop your awareness out of your head and into the heart-space of transformation.

- Ask for the pattern that relates to this experience to emerge. Allow it to be as abstract as possible, so your judging mind does not try to jump in.

- Once you find the pattern, move your awareness to it, and notice how it begins to shift. If you feel like interacting with it, then do so. You can untangle it or perhaps even "blow" on it. The more surprising your impulse the better! Don't expect this pattern to shift in the same way other patterns have shifted. Allowing yourself to be in the moment, will create the best results.

Once you are finished, it is time to calibrate the results. It might be awhile before someone lies to you again, since once you are different, your experiences can show up differently! Perhaps you will now draw people with excellent integrity, or perhaps you will notice that when someone slips up with a deceit, you have no strong reaction. Occasionally, I have watched clients forget about their previous experiences so completely that they don't even remember what the problem was that they had!

VIBRATING INTO LOVE

I once had a client who was ready and wanting to meet her soul mate. She had relationships in the past that for one reason or another never moved beyond a certain point. We talked for a while about the kind of connection that felt strong and true for her. We didn't focus on the details of what kind of job her soul mate should have or how tall he should be. Instead she talked about how open he would be to her; how he would provide attention and intimacy; how connected she would feel in his presence. Then I went to work and selected the vibrations that matched these descriptions. In the space where light and information create patterns, we have access to all possibilities. Thus, all vibrations exist there. As I collected the vibrations she talked about, I moved each into her energy field until she was vibrating with the very essence of what she was looking to create with a soul mate. Two months later she emailed me and told me that she had met someone new and amazing, and was so excited by the deep connection they shared!

Can it be this easy? We live in a world of vibration. Each physical object and each experience have a signature of vibration. You have heard of the Law of Attraction, which says you will draw to you the things that are of your same vibration. This seems to play out with regularity in our world for sure. But creating the vibration that we want in ourselves seems to be the more difficult task. This is where a lot of experimentation and exploration will serve you well. You can collect vibrations from the world of the things you would like to experience. They can come from anywhere: a mountain vista, a warm bubble bath, a relaxing massage, a beautiful symphony, a fragrant lavender bush, a laughing child. Tune in to the world around you and begin collecting vibrations of love, joy, deep serenity, and peace. All of these will tune your unique signature vibration in ways that will allow you to connect even more deeply with these vibrations. The "Becoming the Vibration You Seek" exercise will allow you to connect with the vibration of love that you seek.

EXERCISE

Becoming the Vibration You Seek

- Start with something you really love: a piece of beautiful music, or a bubble bath with candles and rose petals.

- As you relax, imagine being with your most ideal companion. Imagine the laughter or deep trust or deep connected presence that you feel being together.

- Ask for the pattern of this collection of feelings to appear. However it shows up is fine. Some people might feel a tingling or see a glowing crystal ball. There is no right way for it to appear; it will be unique to you.

- Now draw that pattern into your energy field. Allow your current vibration to melt into this new vibration. Notice the new vibration spreading throughout your being.

- Become aware of any aspects of yourself that resist this new vibration. Stay away from any judgment, and just notice.

• Ask for the pattern of this resistance. Gently move your awareness to it. Often you may feel an impulse to envelope this pattern in love and compassion. If so, do not hesitate. Allow this pattern to shift and change as needed.

• Then notice again as the new vibration you are bringing into your being spreads throughout all of who you are—throughout the physical, emotional, mental, and spiritual aspects of you.

• If you notice any additional places of resistance, repeat the process above.

• End by melting your entire being into this new vibration that you have created, feeling fully connected and flush with the love you are vibrating with.

• Now as you move about the world, watch how your experiences begin to match this new vibration. You may even meet others that share this vibration, and find your soul mate in the process!

EXPANDING CONSCIOUSNESS BEYOND THE PERSONAL

Expanding our consciousness brings us into awareness of our full being. As you practice the exercises in this book, your awareness will become fluid and flexible. Eventually, you will be easily living (and even thinking) from your heart-space. As a result, you will experience a different kind of peace that comes from a connection with your whole being and whole awareness. Life is so much more immediate when you live from your heart rather than your head. Once you reach this point, the magical divine simply becomes who you are, rather than something you do. And very naturally you find you can simply *be*.

AN UNEXPECTED GIFT

As I explored the realms of consciousness, I noticed how much I changed in the process without even trying. A miracle that I had not intended occurred when I wasn't looking. I started as an uncertain, left-brained thinker, with questionable self-esteem and many negative voices in my head. Along the way—as I practiced the tools I have shared with you, and as I performed countless sessions for clients—many of my limitations melted away. The negative voices in my head faded. While I still hear them, they are fainter, and don't really seem like me. The meta-rules I used, in order to avoid having to fix my own limitations, seem to have melted them away anyway.

As I lived more and more from my heart-space, not just during sessions but during my everyday life, a sense of graceful movement in the 3-D world became my normal experience. No longer was the world a hostile place, fraught with pending triggers to my self-esteem. I was slowly able to stay completely connected to Source as I moved throughout my life.

This state of grace became apparent as desires began to manifest quite naturally without even trying. The universe and I are one, a connection that simply flows. At this point it barely startles me to think, *Oh, a cup of tea would be lovely*, and to find it already made when I turn the corner to the kitchen. When I notice patterns that I want to shift, they do so without any more than my simple intention that I would like to see them shift. The typical stressors of everyday life still happen, but I am able to negotiate these smoothly and easily. My attention no longer gets stuck in the vortex of dwelling on the glitches of life. I naturally see the world as a magical, fun place to explore and experience.

Most importantly, because I am able to access the spaces beyond the 3-D realm of human form, I am always aware that the human experience I am having is just one aspect of me. As Walt Whitman said, "I am large; I contain multitudes!" With that perspective, my human experience has become a lovely game. Because I am aware of myself as a multi-dimensional being, my human experience is enriched beyond measure! I can experience a full realm of emotions, from ecstatic joy to sweet sadness to empowering rage!

Fully connected to Source and seeing myself as an inventive creator of my experiences, I no longer feel that life happens to me. So I revel in all of it! I find the physical body amazing and miraculous. I enjoy the amazing buzz of a great yoga practice right along with the heightened sensory experience when my body runs a fever. My judgment of what experiences are good or bad dissolves, as I embrace them all.

Immense pleasure comes from the most ordinary places! Enlightenment, it seems, is not about escaping our daily lives, but about finding a deep peace with each ordinary moment. The experience of being human has become a treasured gift now that I have experienced myself beyond the human form.

FROM SEPARATION TO
UNIFIED CONSCIOUSNESS

As if this is not amazing enough, I also find that my journey has progressed beyond my own personal ego concerns, such as wanting to be a great healer to win admiration or wanting to manifest greater abundance to ease my personal struggles. These egoic concerns still arise at times, but I seem to be tapped into a larger consciousness. Somehow I experience myself as linked to everyone; the patterns are all connected and there is no more sense of separation. I never suspected that practicing these tools would shift my view from the personal to an understanding of our connection to the whole. I have become acutely aware that success in transformation is not just an individual endeavor. The next step in transforming ourselves and our world requires co-creating with others.

I feel the urgency these days to share these tools with others, so that more and more of us can experience this personal transformation; as we each do so, the transformation of the whole also occurs. As the global patterns change, we see rapid and fruitful shifts in our world. The revolutions in the Middle East are shining examples of transformation on a larger scale. Old models slip away and new business and political models emerge. This global transformation makes it easier for those embarking on the path of personal transformation, just as each person's personal transformation also empowers the whole. We are interrelated, and we are all contributing to an amazing shift on the Earth. No matter where you are on this amazing path, your contribution helps.

One of the best ways to nurture the process of expanding your consciousness is to get involved in groups and classes where you are mingling with people who are also exploring and expanding their consciousness. Many participants in my workshops have confided that once they return home, there are few if any other people who understand what they are trying to do. Their feeling of isolation makes continuing their studies and explorations more difficult. For this reason, I offer many teleclasses as well as live workshops that can help people stay in the vibration of expansion. And I'm not the only one. There are others who offer groups as well that support transformation.

What is important is to get connected with like-minded people. If you feel a resonance with my work, that's wonderful. If you feel the pull to other classes and teachers, then honor that. You are always your own best guide along your path.

I am looking forward to a world where most people are walking through their lives in their heart-space, seeing the unity and oneness of all; where we all melt into the divine magic that weaves throughout the world, and honor our sacred connections to the Earth and to each other. It is already beginning. Each small step that each of us takes is exponentially multiplied through our combined co-creation. I am honored to take these steps with you.

QUICK REFERENCE GUIDE TO EXERCISES

Some of the following exercises are provided as complimentary mp3 audios to enhance your experience. To download the audio versions, visit www.AlchemyWisdom.com and find the link "Resources." Instructions for downloading will be provided.

Creating Your Meta-Rules   20
Use to discover and quickly short-cut your personal limitations.

Gathering Yourself   30
Use to practice controlling your awareness.

Moving into Your Heart-Space   32
Use to explore and expand your heart awareness. This is the space we create from, and as such, this is one of the most important exercises.

Moving through Your Bodies   34

Use to expand your awareness and improve your control over directing your awareness.

Moving Up and Down   35

Use to expand your awareness and improve your control over directing your awareness.

Dispersing the Emotional Vortex   42

Use to move quickly through painful emotions or fear.

Discovering the Space Between   46

Use to move quickly out of your head and find a neutral perspective. This is also a great tool for accessing the heart-space.

Visiting the Lower World   49

Use to begin to map some spaces in consciousness. Can be simply exploratory, or can be used to gain information or for healing personal issues.

Fear-Busting Rehearsal   69

Use to begin to release fears that are holding you back.

Seeing through the Illusion of Fear   70

Use to face fears and watch them lose their power over you.

Choosing from Your Heart   86

Use to aid you in listening for your inner guidance. This exercise can help you understand what your heart is telling you.

Strengthening Your Connection to Guidance   89
Use to aid you in connecting and listening for your inner guidance.

Finding Patterns   112
Use to find and access the patterns in the hologram that you want to change.

Changing a Health Pattern   116
Use this exercise as the basic process for changing patterns in your hologram.

Shifting Your Money Patterns   121
Use to explore and shift your patterns around money and finances.

Gratitude Meditation   124
This exercise is foundational to creating positive states and emotions. Even though it is presented in the money chapter, it is worth using daily to create ease, grace and happiness throughout your day.

Detaching from Morphic Fields   129
Use when your thoughts and beliefs are a part of a larger cultural or global field.

Finding a New Option   132
Use when you don't like any of the possible solutions you have for an issue or problem.

Moving beyond Your Circle of Awareness   133

Use when you can't imagine a solution to a problem or issue. This exercise is instrumental in expanding your awareness beyond what you currently know.

Completing Your Own Circuits   140

This is an excellent exercise to improve your relationship to yourself and your Source. Not just for manifesting relationships, this tool is an excellent one to use daily to create ease, grace and happiness throughout your day.

The Mirror   142

Use to shift the parts of yourself that are creating unpleasant situations in your life. Even though this is included in the relationship chapter, it can be useful for many issues and problems.

Changing the Patterns that Keep You from Love   144

Use to explore and shift the patterns in your hologram that affect your relationships.

Becoming the Vibration You Seek   147

Use to help you manifest the experiences you want to have. Even though this is included in the relationship chapter, it can be used for manifestation of any kind.

BIBLIOGRAPHY

Braden, Gregg. *Walking Between the Worlds: The Science of Compassion.* Bellevue, WA: Radio Bookstore Press, 1997.

Brennan, Barbara Ann. *Hands of Light: A Guide to Healing Through the Human Energy Field.* New York: Bantam Books, 1988.

Chodron, Pema. *When Things Fall Apart: Heart Advice for Difficult Times.* Boston: Shambhala Publications, 1997.

Dale, Cyndi. *The Subtle Body: An Encyclopedia of Your Energetic Anatomy.* Boulder, CO: Sounds True, 2009.

Goswami, Amit. *The Self-Aware Universe: How Consciousness Creates the Material World.* New York: Tarcher/Putnam, 1993.

Hunt, Valerie V. *Infinite Mind: Science of the Human Vibrations of Consciousness.* Malibu, CA: Malibu Publishing, 1996.

Kraig, Donald Michael. *Modern Magick: Eleven Lessons in the High Magickal Arts.* St. Paul, MN: Llewellyn Publications, 1992.

Losey, Meg Blackburn. *Pyramids of Light: Awakening to Multi-Dimensional Realities.* Andersonville, TN: Meg Blackburn Losey, 2004.

Melchizedek, Drunvalo. *The Ancient Secret of the Flower of Life, Volume 1.* Flagstaff, AZ: Light Technology Publishing, 1998.

——. *The Ancient Secret of the Flower of Life, Volume 2*. Flagstaff, AZ: Light Technology Publishing, 2000.

Mindell, Arnold. *The Quantum Mind and Healing: How to Listen and Respond to Your Body's Symptoms*. Charlottesville, VA: Hampton Roads Publishing, 2004.

Nichols, L. Joseph. *The Soul as Healer: Lessons in Affirmation, Visualization, and Inner Power*. St. Paul, MN: Llewellyn Publications, 2000.

Oschman, James L. *Energy Medicine: The Scientific Basis*. Edinburgh: Churchill Livingstone, 2000.

Pierrakos, Eva. *The Pathwork of Self-Transformation*. New York: Bantam Books, 1990.

Penczak, Christopher. *Ascension Magick: Ritual, Myth and Healing for the New Aeon*. Woodbury, MN: Llewellyn Publications, 2007.

Schlitz, Marilyn, Tina Amorok, and Marc S. Micozzi (Eds.). *Consciousness and Healing: Integral Approaches to Mind-Body Medicine*. St. Louis: Elsevier, 2005.

Scully, Nicki. *Alchemical Healing: A Guide to Spiritual, Physical, and Transformational Medicine*. Rochester, VT: Bear and Company, 2003.

Tiller, William A. *Science and Human Transformation: Subtle Energies, Intentionality and Consciousness*. Walnut Creek, CA: Pavior Publishing, 1997.

——. "Towards a Quantitative Science and Technology that Includes Human Consciousness." First published in *VIA, The Journal of New Thinking for New Action*, 1.4 (2003). Published by Vision-In-Action, www.via-visioninaction.org. http://www.quantrek.org/Technical%20Literature/Tiller_Vision_in_Action_Article_a.pdf.

Tolle, Eckhart. *A New Earth: Awakening to Your Life's Purpose*. New York: Dutton, 2005.

Vaughn-Lee, Llewellyn. *Alchemy of Light: Working with the Primal Energies of Life.* Inverness, CA: The Golden Sufi Center, 2007.

———. *Spiritual Power: How It Works.* Inverness, CA: The Golden Sufi Center, 2005.

———. *Working with Oneness.* Inverness, CA: The Golden Sufi Center, 2002.

ABOUT THE AUTHOR

Jaden Rose Phoenix is the founder of Alchemy Wisdom, a healing arts center. Originally trained as a massage therapist, she realized very quickly that her true interests lay in modern alchemy and consciousness technologies that create fast and effective shifts for her clients and for herself.

She is respected world-wide for her masterful ability to take esoteric or complex information and distill it in a fun and practical way for everyday use, making her learning programs accessible for everyone. With her guidance, the magic of peace and grace are not just for the monks who've meditated for 20 years, but are easily mastered by everyday folk.

A teacher and coach for over twenty years, she spent the last eight years studying and presenting transformational techniques and tools in workshops nationwide. During that time she developed a method called Holographic Healing™, a system of transformation that she delivers to individuals and to groups via teleconference, as well as a workshop called Holographic Principles™, which she teaches nationally and internationally to participants who want to learn these powerful methods.

As a co-founder of the *International Center for Consciousness Medicine*, Jaden is passionate about creating opportunities to share and explore knowledge in the area of consciousness studies. She continues to develop transformational technologies that allow people to tap into new vibrations and energies that promote radical change in their lives.

Her current website is www.AlchemyWisdom.com.

Also available from

JADEN ROSE PHOENIX

WORKSHOPS

Holographic Principles, Level 1 and 2

8 Keys to Claiming the Power and Magic of Your Limitless Self

- Learn the consciousness keys to accessing grace and miracles in your everyday life.
- Experience hands on opportunities for practicing with each of these keys.
- Develop an individual approach to use when reprogramming your hologram.
- Learn strategies to transform your life, easily clear limitations, improve relationships, face everyday challenges with greater ease, and experience peace and contentment regardless of what is occurring around you.
- Learn to embody the space of rapid transformation
- Understand the ancient traditions and the modern science of consciousness, as Jaden weaves magic, alchemy and eastern wisdom throughout.
- Bring the magic of conscious creation into your life in practical ways.
- Experience and understand the potential, power, and magic of claiming your limitless self.

For current list of locations and dates, see
www.AlchemyWisdom.com.

Also available from

JADEN ROSE PHOENIX

AUDIOS

Consciousness Magic Study Groups

Consciousness Magic is a series of study groups to help you use consciousness effectively in your life. Detailed information and exercises are included that greatly expand the basic information in this text.

Set A: Understanding the Basics

Audio #1: Energy vs Consciousness
Audio #2: The Role of Intent
Audio #3: Finding the Point of Power
Audio #4: Finding the Pattern You Want to Change
Audio #5: Subduing the Cry of the Ego, or Using Meta-Rule Sets

Set B: Basic Transformation Skills

Audio #6: Changing What You Don't Want
Audio #7: Creating What You Do Want
Audio #8: Accessing What You Cannot Imagine
Audio #9: Adding Dimensional Shifts
Audio #10: Basics of Healing and Manifestation

Set C: Intermediate Transformation Skills

Audio #11: Working on Yourself
Audio #12: Working at a Distance
Audio #13: Creating Lasting Changes
Audio #14: Working with Relationships
Audio #15: In-depth Work with Dimensional Shifts

For updated product offerings, see www.AlchemyWisdom.com.

CPSIA information can be obtained at www.ICGtesting.com
Printed in the USA
265938BV00001B/3/P